Other Land:

Contemporary Poems
on Wales and Welsh-American Experience

Other Land:

Contemporary Poems
on Wales and Welsh-American Experience

Edited by David Lloyd

Parthian
The Old Surgery
Napier Street
Cardigan
SA43 1ED

www.parthianbooks.co.uk

First published in 2008
© the authors 2008
This collection © Parthian 2008
All Rights Reserved

ISBN 978-1-905762-22-4

Cover design by Lucy Llewellyn
Inner design and typesetting by www.lloydrobson.com
Printed and bound by Dinefwr Press, Llandybïe, Wales

Published with the financial support of the Welsh Books
Council

British Library Cataloguing in Publication Data
A cataloguing record for this book is available from the
British Library

Contents

Anne Stevenson

Introduction

Many American poets have written about Wales, often after brief visits. But *Other Land: Contemporary Poems on Wales and Welsh-American Experience* presents poets with an American background who have written in sustained and considered ways about the Welsh culture, landscape, and people. These are not 'occasional poets' or tourist poets who sentimentalize or glamourize Welsh history or immigrant experience. A poem's subject might be a person (such as Jon Dressel's alter-ego Dai), a town (as with Joseph Clancy's poems set in Aberystwyth), a landscape (the hills of Anne Stevenson's Powys), a family story (Denise Levertov's poems on her mother's childhood), a Welsh poet (William Virgil Davis's 'First Light,' in memory of R S Thomas), a megalithic monument (William Greenway's 'At Arthur's Stone'), voices from the past (Sarah Kennedy's poems drawing from 18th century domestic manuscripts), or Welsh myth (Margaret Lloyd's rendering of the Arthurian material, Margot Farrington's treatment of the selkie story, or my own merging of parts of the *Mabinogi* with elements of American popular culture). Whatever the subject, the poets' explorations are informed and energized by deep connection, in some cases over the course of a lifetime. Despite my interest in presenting the ways certain American poets respond to aspects of Wales, my overarching criterion for inclusion is that each poem succeed, first and foremost, as a poem.

Because seven of the contributors are Welsh-descended, immigrant experience and the process of acculturation as well as direct experience of Wales figure in this anthology. While Jon Dressel, William Greenway, Denise Levertov, Margaret Lloyd and I have a parent, parents, or grandparents who were born in Wales, William Virgil Davis and Sarah Kennedy's Welsh ancestors emigrated in the more distant past. Margot Farrington's long-time interest in the literatures of Ireland, Scotland and Wales particularly centered on Wales after she heard a Welsh poet read at a library near her home in Brooklyn. Two of the poets connect to Wales by long-time residence: Anne Stevenson – born in England of American parents but raised in the United States – now divides her time between homes in England and in north Wales; Joseph Clancy, a New Yorker of Irish descent who is also an accomplished translator of Welsh poetry and prose, moved to Aberystwyth in 1990 after his retirement from Marymount Manhattan College in 1990.

Despite their varied connections to Wales, the ten poets in this anthology communicate a self-conscious and often ironic sense of belonging elsewhere: Wales remains for them a distinctly separate, if familiar, 'other land'. To varying degrees the poets share William Greenway's sense that in Wales 'Things are different' ('Welsh Courier Braves Daylight'). There are many, often comic, moments in these poems where difference confronts a character or the speaker, as when the eight-year-old 'pure Missouri' boy in Jon Dressel's 'The Holy Well' tells his father that what they are looking at cannot be a well because 'There's no bucket', wells being, in an American context, purely utilitarian.

While this Introduction, the Acknowledgements, and the Notes for the poems follow British rather than American spelling and punctuation conventions, the poems themselves follow conventions according to each poet's preference. It seemed contrary to the spirit of the anthology to insist on a British standard for American forms of speech, versions of what poet William Carlos Williams termed 'the American idiom', or an American standard for poems written in and about Wales by poets who have long resided in Britain.

The poems of *Other Land*, finally, are as concerned with degrees of difference as they are with connectedness; they're as much about cross-currents in sensibilities and preoccupations – and poetic idioms – as they are about 'the matter of Wales'.

David Lloyd
Syracuse, USA

William Greenway

William Greenway's eighth collection is *Fishing at the End of the World* (Word Press, 2005). His seventh collection, *Ascending Order*, won the 2004 Ohioana Best Book of Poetry Prize (University of Akron Press Poetry Series). His poems have appeared in *American Poetry Review*, *Georgia Review*, *Poetry*, *Poetry Northwest*, *Prairie Schooner*, *Shenandoah* and *The Southern Review*. He has won the Helen and Laura Krout Memorial Poetry Award, the Larry Levis Editors' Prize from *Missouri Review*, the Open Voice Poetry Award from The Writer's Voice, the State Street Press Chapbook Competition, an Ohio Arts Council Grant, and was 1994 Georgia Author of the Year. He is Professor of English at Youngstown State University, where he was awarded a Distinguished Professorship in Teaching and two in Scholarship.

Otherworld

Even the dogs in West Kerry know that the Otherworld exists and that
to be in and out of it constantly is the most natural thing in the world.

Nuala Ní Dhomhnaill

This is where a woman fell
to her death the other day,
climbing the cliff.
They found her face-up, spread-eagled
on the sand, as if she'd been ravished
by a god, or tried to fly.
On this rare hot day in Wales,
hang-gliders fill the Down above,
each aspiring Icarus fluttering
silken, colored wings like the butterflies
in the gorse, which smells, the guidebooks
always say, of "desiccated coconut,"
like the ghost of some tropical isle.
She scaled these strata of seafloor
crowded up into the air until they grew
green and strewn with sheep on top,
where we walk and flirt with the edge
that boys clamber down to fish the ledges.
And though the border collies
bark at azure sea and sky, and try
to herd us back to safety,
as if they hear something we don't
out there, we lean and listen.

Pit Pony

There are only a few left, he says,
kept by old Welsh miners, souvenirs, like
gallstones or gold teeth, torn
from this "pit," so cold and wet my
breath comes out a soul up
into my helmet's lantern
beam, anthracite walls running,
gleaming, and the floors iron-rutted
with tram tracks, the almost pure
rust that grows and waves like
orange moss in the gutters of water
that used to rise and drown.
He makes us turn all lights off, almost
a mile down. While children scream,
I try to see anything, my hand touching
my nose, my wife beside me – darkness palpable,
velvet sack over our heads, even the glow
of watches left behind. This is where
they were born, into this nothing, felt
first with their cold noses for the shaggy
side and warm bag of black
milk, pulled their trams for twenty
years through pitch, past birds
that didn't sing, through doors
opened by five-year-olds who sat
in the cheap, complete blackness listening
for steps, a knock. And they

died down here, generation after
generation. The last one, when it
dies in the hills, not quite blind, the mines
closed forever, will it die strangely? Will it
wonder dimly why it was exiled from the rest
of its race, from the dark flanks of the soft
mother, what these timbers are that hold up
nothing but blue? If this is the beginning
of death, this wind, these stars?

Welsh Courier Braves Daylight

– for John

The book we ordered didn't come in.
It didn't get put
on the van, she says.
Maybe next week.

Things are different here.
We order our turkey
from Rhys the Meat
who hands it to us
in a flurry of feathers,
though he doesn't know why,
or what Thanksgiving is.
The little watchmaker,
in his element
of Dickensian ticking,
declines to tackle
my electric watch.
The fishmonger says,
I don't know.
Crabs is crabs.
The kind with little legs.

Out on the blue bay
draining to low tide,
fishing boats bob
to find bottom;
wild ponies have picked the gate
to eat our garden,
and sheep wander the roads
like blown batting.
Our e-mail won't work,
and for fax and photocopy
we go down to the village
to the model train store.
I watch the tiny cars trace rails
through matchbox coal towns
and pipe-cleaner trees.

We're living here this year
five time zones away
from all we thought,
and if we miss something
we've learned to let it go,
to have another pint,
knowing whatever it is
just might come on the van
next week, or around the cape
if the seas are mild,
or on muleback
if the snows don't clog the pass.

Worm's Head

Halfway up Rhossili Down,
the fight turns serious,
and I, as usual, go back,
leave you to climb the rest
of the bare flank alone.
I sit in our room with a view,
and because I've never wanted you more,
here, on the double bed, I try to spot you
up on the bouldered moonscape,
somewhere high above the sea,
though my eyes, bat-blind
at the best of times, can't make you out.

Waiting, I walk the flat path
out to the head the Vikings
called the *wurm*, dragon, like the carved
prows of their ships sailing away.
Looking back over my shoulder
to watch the body you're walking over,
the bracken bloody in November evening light,
I pray the thin membrane
we've known about for years won't finally give,
me not there to hold you,
to brush the hair from your white, sleeping face.

Walking back, everything reminds me
of my fear – my shadow shooting ahead
and over the cliff, the single seagull
on symbolic ledge, the boy
fishing the dark, rising tide
from the crumbling rocks below,
wind scuffing the sea as if to mend
a puncture. The ram that's broken through
the smallest tear in the hedge, and though
alone with all that long, lovely grass,
runs desperately and aimlessly
in the space that is suddenly everywhere.

Halloween in Wales

Not a pumpkin to be seen
here twenty years ago, but now they leer
from everywhere at us, who knew
corn sheaves and covered bridges,
tree-lined country roads like tunnels
through flame, bobbing
winesaps, and "Little
Orphant Annie" sweeping up
the supper crumbs.

But let them have their goblins
back, who invented banshees, witches
hovering on the heaths, the stags'
heads of ancient Druids, wicker men
and Green Man golems, fairies, the flibbertigibbet
of bats. God knows they have
the props: fog and mist and
moaning wind, castles chock-a-block
with ghosts and all the ghastly forms
of flesh, of what we feel and fear
inside, down the road the cottage where
a hangman hanged himself,
and the hill where an archdruid burned
a baby, offspring of his sin.

But we miss the children begging candy,
the comic danger of stumbling spooks
believing completely what they've become,
my sister in a tutu, a cape that finally
let me fly, the certain knowledge
that sweetness dwelt in every house.
Here, we wait for Guy Fawkes, stuffed
and mortal man, the Old Guy children ask
a penny for. To celebrate his not
killing when he meant to kill,
they gather all the scraps,
carry them to the highest spots,
then pile them up and put on top
a man of straw and light the fires
and dance and whoop, and every hill
burns like a baby.

At Arthur's Stone

– for Gilbert

They say on simmer dim this stone will stand
then walk the long slope down to Burry to drink.
At the winter solstice, hand-in-hand

for now, the truce between us holding for a while,
we walk the frosted rusty red
of autumn fern, past a moldering pile

of wild Welsh pony bones
to see this grave of an early king,
a stone balanced long ago on other stones.

We touch its blotched, gray flank
as millions have, for luck,
as though solidity and poise, its blank

face could cure us of our yearnings, keep
our lives together till we die.
Nearby's a cairn of those like us, a heap

of stones too numerous to name, too small
to walk, that marks the grave of men
who dragged or sailed it here to rest on tall

and humpbacked Cefyn Bryn, to overlook the bay
of cockle sands that glisten when the tide is out,
and be the shrine of girls who came to lay

milk-soaked honey cake upon the ground
before this altar stone,
and crawl three times around –

if her love were true, he would appear,
transported from whatever distant place,
easing through the mist to meet her here.

The moon comes up behind a pony white
as a unicorn, the sun goes down
and pinks the sky and bay before the night

recalls this postcard from the past.
Too far away to see the cars
and houses with their shipwreck masts

of washing poles and satellite dishes,
we might be a pelted pair of ancient,
shivering, short-lived, walking wishes

staring at the mound where we will lie.
And every longest day, the sun
will squint between the lids of sea and sky

that never close, and from this height –
as we dream our centuries of thirst
through the long, dying light –

like a mote in an eye that cannot blink,
the stone of one who lost his love
will walk to the sea to drink.

Llyn y Fan Fach

– for Nigel

It means in Welsh the small lake of the high
ground, or something, all their places
hallowed with words of what or where or why –

*St. Mary's Church in a hollow by the white
hazel close to the rapid whirlpool,*
etc., or stories of what might

have been. Here, a woman with a golden comb
rose from a lake in a lap of mountains
to let a poor and lonely farmer take her home,

only to return, when she had paid her debt
of love, taking his sheep and oxen back
to the waters closed forever on a story of regret.

All of it meaning something else down deep,
like the forest underneath our feet that day
already up to the chapter on peat

and climbing on to the coal and steep
diamond denouement. We'd hiked
the gravel path through red-daubed sheep

halfway up Wales to the highest view,
and though we've always told ourselves
You never regret the things you do,

only the things you don't, that bare hill
glowered down at us until we took
our boots off, stuck our feet into the chill

fairy woman's world, though not stripping
to swim, to join our Welsh friend blowing
and splashing, a young and dripping

Welsh Whitman, and we declined to climb to where
the brow of mountain beetled over all
of lonely Wales that clear, rare,

cloudless day, and back we walked without the end
of the story, talking of the folktales of America
instead, telling our impulsive friend

how Paul Bunyan made the Mississippi with his ax
and ox, of Johnny Appleseed, the pioneers,
the tiny graves beside the rutted tracks

of wagon trains, the tragedies of travel,
and hearing through ourselves, in the interval of words,
the mewling of sheep and the gnawing of gravel.

The Train to Neath

Like lantern blur through fog, we ride
across the coal-dust river to
the cinder bank of the other side,

almost disembodied, dead,
gliding along aloof and looking
over garden walls and into potting sheds,

past flowered council housing shades
to rooms where peat fires smoke and photos
on the mantels craze and fade.

The backs hold sticks of broken winter frames
whose shards of hothouse glass infect
a knacker's yard of furniture gone lame

after the mines were closed. Now coal
is scarce, the union hall is used
for bingo, everyone is on the dole.

We watch as lovers mime good-byes into the dark;
the conductor stamps our tickets with his cross,
or ankh – he thinks we want to disembark,

instead of this continued opportunity
of sliding past and looking at
eye-level life with insular impunity,

like the cushioned joints we barely feel,
the rails so close but still detached,
thumping out their muffled pairs of wheels

like heartbeats under wool, a demi-death –
the double panes of windows holding back
our words but showing us our breath.

Power in the Blood

Cleaning out my father's office
I kept humming his favorite hymn,
"Throw Out the Lifeline."
Maybe I saw it in a yellowed
sermon he never got to preach.
At his funeral, I lasted till the second verse –
When we've been there ten thousand years,
bright shining as the sun.

Here on the coast of Wales,
where it started with my grandfather
in chapels up the smoky valleys,
on cliffs I've learn the need
of clefts in rock, anything to block
the wind, I've seen the lifeboat
flume to the waves and heard, from a room
of whisky and candlelight,
the boom of the lifeline rocket
flaring in the storm.

Are you washed in the blood? we'd ask
each other every Sunday night
while the rest of the heathen world
watched *The Wizard of Oz*,
or the Beatles on Ed Sullivan,
or sat in a bar, or wrote their poems.
Monday morning found my mother
back on her knees, scrubbing, scrubbing,
slapping me for muddy shoes, insolent
prints on the polished mahogany.

Even now, I'm contemptuous
of those who try to make their own religion,
hate Sunday nights: the lonely, straying
ones who end alone and childless
in furnished, rented rooms, writing
letters to the editor, or poems,
peculiar, faithless souls who sing
late into the night the drunken hymns
of childhood, where tomorrow's sun
may never shine, and clothes, when washed
in blood, grow white as snow.

Fancy View

We have lunch in the crater
of a green moonscape,
guessing what – glacier, bomb,
the forestry service? – has made it
then soothed it over
like a nightmare putting green,
and planted around the lip
of this cup holding our picnic table,
a golden picket of young birches,
a fort I would have loved as a boy
with long October afternoons to spend.

Up a steep climb is the "Fancy View,"
through blue haze the rust of autumn
on hills like the Georgia Smokies
where my grandfather settled because,
red dirt and all, they reminded him
of the hills of Wales he saw as a boy
coming up, at the end of the day,
in a cage from the mine.

On the walk down is a plaque
drilled into golden stone
showing beneath us the squirm
of mines, the hills around us slag tips,
telling how boys woke at four
and walked five miles in the dark
to pull all day on their knees
through tunnels the sleds of coal,
and, going home, played rugby
by the pit-light of the moon,
how hostlers fed the horses
in the cold down there,
only bringing them up for strikes,
then taking them back down for good.

Our faces lie on the glass
of a few old, smoky photographs
of machines, mustached men
in bowler hats and suits,
and black-faced boys too small
for the miners' lamps they wear,
and we walk more carefully, lightly,
back to the car as if our weight
might crush the tunnels riddling
underneath our feet,
keeping everything down forever.

Footpaths

Jon Anderson, my Jo Jon
We've climbed the hill together,
And many a canty day, Jon,
We've had with one another.

Robert Burns

This is why we came, these tracks
through farmyard and field, around
rusted harrows as the farmers work,
their border collies crazy-eyed at us
as two more things to organize, direct,
although our feet already trace
the steps of sheep and cows, between
the green pools of slurry, here
where fence nor nothing private
can stop us legally, because the dead,
lying in the churchyards of these valleys,
have stamped a seal into this clay
and put a stile over every obstacle.

Even in dreams, I follow
a stenciled yellow arrow on the walls
of train stations, into toilets, over stiles,
through a window into an alley,
nowhere I can't go, until the trees
thicken and I can't fit between or through
contractions of a farmhouse window,
my body inside, my head left stuck
on the sill, cooling like a pie.

We've walked hundreds of miles like this;
our maps, weary at the fold,
we point like dueling compasses,
our shadows hesitating
on the sundial of a field,
our feet always after another
dotted line or hedged-in lane.
We know how long a wrong turn takes,
have come to hate the forks,
and tire of saying *the road not taken*.

We travel well, you say;
it's home where we get lost.
On the tops of hills, our breathing slow,
we've learned the price of every view,
and measure our desire against
the steeper climb, the even steeper fall,
where the knees almost want to fail,
give in, to just let go and run,
as if we'd be able to stop.

The colors this November
still have a way to go,
and though the summer was warmer
than ever before, the winter
has taken no offense so far.
Has a winter ever never happened?
They say there's a valley near

no frost has ever touched,
and though we have no map,
why should that stop us now?
As long as we can see at least the ghosts
of other steps across the field,
let's take this path through woods,
and the long climb over the hill.

Jon Dressel

Jon Dressel – whose maternal grandparents were Welsh immigrants from Llanelli – grew up in the Saint Louis industrial suburb of Granite City, Illinois. He taught American Literature and Creative writing at Webster University in Saint Louis, and from 1976 to 1998 was director of the American Programme and later the M A Degree in Creative Writing at Trinity College, Carmarthen. From 1980 to 2005 he was owner of Dressel's Pub in Saint Louis, the largest Welsh pub in North America, now owned by his son. He has published six collections of poetry (three in collaboration with the Welsh poet T James Jones): *Hard Love and a Country* (Christopher Davies, 1977); *Cerddi Ianws* (Gomer Press, 1979); *Out of Wales* (Alun Books, 1984); *The Road to Shiloh* (Gomer Press, 1994); *Wyneb yn Wyneb/Face to Face* (Gomer Press, 1997); and *Rhubanau Dur/Ribbons of Steel* (illustrated chapbook, Gomer Press, 2000). *Cerddi Ianws*, adapted into Welsh in collaboration with T James Jones, was unanimously awarded the Bardic Crown at the National Eisteddfod of Wales at Caernarfon in 1979, but disqualified when the authors revealed their collaboration. In 1996 he was inducted into Yr Orsedd Y Beirdd (The Order of the Bards) at the National Eisteddfod at Llandeilo.

The Holy Well

We walked down the beach at dusk
for a mile and a half, the shrunken
tidal Tywi on our left, around
the darkening points, our feet hardly

knowing the tautly rippled sand, gulls
thinning out, to the path to the well.
My wife was winded. She took to a bench,
gathering breath for home, while I led

our son, eight that day and pure
Missouri, up the soft, dark path.
A gate, and down stone stairs and there
it was, a gothic arch, its symmetry

gone, set low in the bank at our
feet. That's not a well, he said.
It is, it is, and there must
have been a hermit once, I told him.

Then let me jump in. No, it's too
deep. He tossed a stick. See, it's not
far, the water's just there.
And so it was, black as loam, as

a sound in fresh night. It's not
a well, he said. There's no bucket.
It's been a long time, I said;
besides, it was more a place to go,

like your hideout under the bush near
the alley in Saint Louis. He looked
around, felt the stone, bent and tossed
a second sprig. Then we sat down.

Synopsis of the Great Yanklo-Welsh Novel

– Apologies to Harri Webb

There's Uncle Rhys, see, a great
ruined nose of a man, soaked to his bunions
with ale; Carnegie's shills recruit him
to bring rollers to America and the first
lad he hooks is his little brother Ben,
given to choirs but hankering for cash
and air beyond Llanelli; Ben goes over,
toils in Pennsylvania, sends for fair
Elizabeth, who takes the cash for the
ticket and visits all her kinfolk;
Ben works six more months, sends a ticket
this time, Elizabeth comes, they get
married in Bethlehem, renounce the Queen,
Ben goes on strike, gets scabbed, agitates
west, acquiring children and knowledge
of America, earns a music degree
in his spare time, leads three choirs,
never makes enough to get shut of the mill,
dies of flu and grit in Illinois, bequeaths
a ton of hymns and a thousand Yankee dollars;
the older children leave school and work,
Elizabeth husbands pennies but never takes
in wash, the girls marry well, no Welsh
boys for them, but the grandsons get
a potent dose of Mam; one day Jon, short
for Jones, comes to Llanelli, on a whim,
aged 27 at the sloshed-out end of a con-
tinental tour; he has a religious ex-
perience on Copperworks Road, chords sound,
he knows who he is; he sells the family

business, begins to write poetry, comes
back for eisteddfodau; finally he brings
the wife and children (Elizabeth and Ben)
to live in Llansteffan, scrounges the keep
importing students from the States, begins
to learn Welsh, not a bad accent either,
all those years with Mam, misses only the
Italian cooking in America, gets that
by driving to Swansea, takes to wearing
a coarse tweed cap, walks Elizabeth and Ben round
the village at dusk (the movie version ends
here, with 'Welcome in the Hillsides' fading
into 'Hen Wlad fy Nhadau' as they cross
a small stone bridge in the company of a dog).

Why I Live in Llansteffan

A condition of being American
is to remember the Nineteenth Century;
my father missed being born in it
by only a couple of years but grew
up in its backwash in a big white frame
farmhouse in Greene County, Illinois,
where the earth lies glacial-flat for leagues
and dark and fecund as a plough's sweet dream;
Yankees and Germans, my dad's side were,
and they kept a tidy place, complete with
a brace of maiden aunts who gathered eggs
and plucked wrung chickens and a bachelor
uncle, born cantankering, who studied
dentistry in Saint Louis, pulled teeth
for a week, locked the office and came home
to rock on the verandah till he died,
four decades on, in total disagreement;
when my dad finally left he didn't go
far, just to town to start a dairy; we
went back every Sunday, as to a shrine
or source, and in summers I spent weeks,
rode the combine at wheat-time, caught rabbits,
lay in the loft of the great red barn
and breathed the enormous aroma
of the hay; it wasn't exactly Fern Hill,
what with the prairie, but it was what I had,
and it occurs to me often lately here
in Llansteffan that perhaps Greene County,
Illinois, has rendered situation
in this place plausible; if I was a stickler
on this Welsh roots business I'd be living
in Llanelli, but my father's were a stubborn

people too, and having got to America first,
they had the farm, and their say with me;
that's one way to look at it; on the other
hand, the last word, there and here, is land.

A Bedtime Story

What finally happened was this:
he came back to Wales with a
handful of his own and a passel
of Indians; squaws, of course,
a few less of braves, and a
sprinkling of papeese; they beached
their boats and made their way
into the hills of Gwynedd,
travelling by night and holing
up by day; they endured for
three centuries, Indian lore,
etc., eating roots and berries,
hunting a little, and murmuring
to Manitou; vague rumors spread
of a tribe of Indian Welshmen,
with dark skin, straight black hair,
and words like 'ugh' and 'how' in their
vocabulary; they had the Indian eyesight
and from their hills they saw it all,
the burning of Deganwy, the business
at Cilmeri, Glyndŵr at Corwen,
Harlech, and the last; they watched
the Tudor progression to Bosworth,
and knew it was time; they built it
huge, a cross between a canoe
and a coracle, put it in the Mawddach
as the tide turned one full moon
and paddled it back to Alabama;
for seven years they trekked due
north, reaching the Arctic Circle
in the month they called Hydref, 1492;
on its eleventh night they revelled,

and on the twelfth, after
an Italian and a scurvy gang
of Spaniards had planted a flag
on a sunny beach far southwards,
they doused their fires, smoked
a final pipeful, and lay down,
glad, to meet their fates,
which came, in dreams, like ice and wolves.

Note from a Soldier

It's big time
no doubt
and who wouldn't

be flattered by
such cosmic
hoopla, all those

bards and minstrels,
frogs and wops
and krauts, even

the limeys
getting in
on the whoopee,

slipping me a
posthumous
Victoria Cross,

Hollywood,
Broadway,
serials on the

goggle-box,
cult-loads
of college kids

mad for the
paperbacks,
the sidekick from

Oz with a show
of his own?
Hell yes, pizzazz,

I can take it
like the next
man, we need it,

it helps us
to understand
Freud. Still,

it's my life
that they're
mucking about

with, and I
often think
back on it,

given a mind,
how I got
smart with horses

and tactics from
the Romans,
raised my troop,

travelled light
and covered
ground, gave them

hell for leather
on the Brython
frontier, pulverized

the Picts in what
they now call
Scotland, slammed

the Saxons silly
on the hill
at Badon, they were

bloody barbarians,
VC or no,
and put the West

off limits for
nearly fifty
years. Yes, we

were Welshmen,
we knew how
to fight, and

we took on the
bastards who
were other than

us, time after
time, whenever
they looked to be

hot for our turf.
We were good,
I won't deny it,

but it was no
big deal, I mean
there wasn't

all that razzamatazz
with Magic Man
and Supersword,

hordes of pretenders
hobbling off to
the hernia ward,

Lady Scuba-Dooba
bubbling up
from the lake,

neuter Goody-
Two-Shoes panting
after mystic

goblets, Mafia
half-sister
and punk nephew

on vendetta,
the boat for
Apple Island

pushing off from
Armageddon,
the bug-eyed

cock-and-bull
shebang. We
rode and fought

and drank, better
than most, we
made it with the

local farm-girls
as we could,
and in our turns

we bled and died.
Madison Avenue
took it from

there. They hyped
it till it
came. It slew them

in Peoria. Sometimes
I damn near
believe it myself.

Two Hoots for a Huntress

It was flesh from
flower as the
story goes but

to assert cold
nature in
the flesh seems

wrong, does not
do justice
to the pistil

in spring sun;
it was simply
flesh without

a carnal story,
come of age
from elsewhere,

for what that
might be worth;
still, it knew

a stud-man when
it saw one,
I say it was

Lleu who had
the cold
within, who

thought, then
felt, a diff-
erence, who

went limp from
contemplation
of her origins

in bloom; so
on came Gronw,
hot from his

kill and ignorant
as blood; he
must have been

good, she kept
him extra
nights, and if

he found her
less than
lusty nothing

in the transcript
shows it;
what they did

next is not to
be admired, yet
human enough,

considering
the context;
the truth con-

fessed to Lleu
and Uncle
Gwydion might

have zapped her,
might have run
her back through

flower all the
way to mud;
so she chose to

try divorce,
Brythonic-
style, and Lleu

could hardly
wait to lace
his impotence

with sappiness,
to spill his
fatal beans,

to almost earn
his spear,
posturing like

a schoolboy on
his guardian
taboos; even so,

it wasn't murder,
it was only
eaglification,

a rotten go but
curable if you
know the right

englynwr; what
Gronw proved was
that a stud can

be a fink, making
like all blame
was hers, it was

blarney, and so
blatant that it
couldn't fool a

stone; and as for
her, well, cold
men judged her,

and were still
half god enough
to make it stick,

yet they blew
it in the end,
it was she who

got the harder
consolation
out of metaphor,

got to be the
thing on wing
below the dreams

of eagles, taking
what it has to
in the darkness

it belongs to,
taking it whole,
spitting back,

in time, the
unconvertible,
the scrap that

gives no heat,
the residual
ball of scruff,

that each fierce
heart in flower
finally knows.

Dai, Live

Prytherch is dead. We have no right
to doubt it, let alone dispute. We must
contend with men we have in sight,

like Dai here, who is clean
as dirt. The rumor in the pub
is that he hasn't been seen

out of that ripening outfit
since the Investiture. It may
be a form of protest, though it

seems more likely, ten pints down,
he's just too whipped to shuck that
wind-grey coat, every button gone,

peel those frazzling sweaters, rife with him
and earth, let those grime-stiff trousers
fall, or try to fall, before things dim.

Too whipped, perhaps, to kick those mud-
brindled boots to a corner, or toss
that crust of a cap to a bed-

post, if he has one. No farmer, Dai,
he digs around the village, roads,
sewers, God knows what, digs all day,

digs everywhere, turns up pints,
grubs of coins for the slots, studies men
who commute to Carmarthen, nods, squints,

grunts a little rugby, weathers at his end
of the bar like a cromlech, drones
like the surf when those with more voice bend

the last elbow in hymn, leaves alone
with a guttural wave, boulders into night,
a man-shape hulking like an age of stone,

that knows no women, but lives with what it knows,
hard as breath, or a December rose.

Note to a Character

Dai i was hoping to write my traditional
return to wales poem featuring you since
you do have this uncanny knack for being
the first person i see in the village but
there's been a lot of comment about your
kind lately and how you're sort of a crea-
ture of pink romantic blinders or if not
quite that certainly an edifice construct-
ed out of all proportion to its base or if
not quite that at least the last of a species
about which nothing much can be said but that
anyway i was walking the meadow path to the
pub still feeling missouri like lead in my
jet lag when I saw this gaunt black dog half
wolfhound half god knows what coming on it was
strange and fierce and flashing tongue
and fang for a moment i thought i was in
an old sherlock holmes movie there's fantasia
for you boyo but then i saw you close behind
risen from dirt as ever stubbling through
the drouth-scythed field a limp black rabbit
or something in your hand it was dead of course
by dog or sling or snare or whatever i haven't
talked to you since it doesn't matter i just
waved and passed by resolute as odysseus
fast to my mast of resistance to metaphor
the pub was mobbed i nursed a pint of mild
made off about ten took my time walking home
brewed a cup of bovril read a little betjeman
watched the tv closedown had a pee and went to bed.

Dai on Holiday

Dai, you startled me, I had been away
six months, back to Missouri, and when
I came into the pub there you were,
in a tweed jacket looking like a thing
exhumed, a white shirt soiled as Job's
boiled sheet, trousers from a dead Sunday
suit, shapeless, held, barely, by a thick
belt gathering without the help of loops,
and shoes, mud-bronzed, in place of boots;
a quantum change, but of the village,
even so; it was that thing on your head,
that cockeyed halo of a crumpled blue
beret, that did me in; it was not
some soldiered surplus from the market,
but Basque, or French, apache, rakish, wise,
reeking of bistros, women's necks, and wine;
and you'd shaved; you face was strangely
white; you'd gashed, and stanched, your chin; still,
the truth was there, fifty-nine years of weather,
forty-three of ale, the man-virgin eyes,
alien, fierce, intact, beneath the brow's mute
crease on crease; they fixed on me; you nodded,
silently smiled, parting your lips till the dreg
of your fag, a finger-stub of ash, hung,
about to flower, from your toothless upper
gum; I stood beside you, dumb; 'he's on
holiday', whispered someone later, in a crowd.

Children, Night, Llansteffan

Walking on my own through the village
after supper, down the long lengths
of empty street between lights,
towards the top of the hill where
the castle road begins its half-mile run
to a dead end, I see them there, in the
wash of light from the pub, the shop,
the candy store, around their totem,
the phone booth, tall, transparent, lit;
two or three, the oldest, crowd in,
while the rest, even the smallest
who don't yet know the need, move
restless, magnetized, around; those
inside call, where? Carmarthen?
Llanybri, a mile away? anywhere
but here. Anywhere but here.
We arrive; my own join the fringe.
I sometimes think my forty years
might rouse the tongue to speak to them,
most of whom will never see Vienna
or Honolulu, and tell them it's
all right, that some of us who have at last
come glad for silence, shrunken, here,
to the dark of Wales by sea and owl.
It's no good, for we come, of course,
from having sound and glitter, after years.
The call ends; they move off, slowly,
from the booth's cold light, one amorphous
creature, murmuring, towards the dark
of the bus shelter, till time to go home.

Denise Levertov

Denise Levertov (1923-1997) was born in Ilford, England. Her mother was Welsh and her father an Anglican priest who had been raised as an Hasidic Jew in Germany. In 1947, Levertov married an American writer, Mitchell Goodman, and they moved to the United States in 1948. She taught at numerous American universities, primarily as a visiting writer, and authored more than 20 books of poetry, criticism, and translations, including *The Sands of the Well* (New Directions, 1996), *Poems 1960-1967* (New Directions, 1983) and *Poems 1968-1972* (New Directions, 1987). Levertov was a scholar at the Radcliffe Institute for Independent Study and a member of the American Institute of Arts and Letters. Among her many awards are the Lenore Marshall Prize for poetry, a Guggenheim Fellowship, the Elmer Holmes Bobst Award, the Shelley Memorial Award, the Robert Frost Medal, the Lannan Award, and a National Institute of Arts and Letters grant.

The Sea Inland

Heather, bracken, the tall Scotch Firs.
There on the mountain, as the wind
came and went in the trees, she could hear
the sea. Closing her eyes she watched it
leaping upon the strand and slowly
returning into itself, tumbling the shingle with it,
to leap again, the over and over
rush, leap forward, and slow withdrawal.
And watched seaweed sway in the pools,
and stretches of wet sand reflect
a gleam of jade as the waves
poised before plunging.
All this she heard and saw on the mountain,
days when there was no school –
long before I was born – as I do now
under Douglas Firs in a western land
long after her death, my now, her then
intermingled as vision and sound
mingle, and what is fleeting and what remains
outside of time.

An Arrival (North Wales, 1897)

The orphan arrived in outlandish hat,
proud pain of new button boots.
Her moss-agate eyes
photographed views of the noonday sleepy town
no one had noticed. Nostrils flaring,
she sniffed odors of hay and stone,
                    absence of Glamorgan coaldust,
and pasted her observations quickly
into the huge album of her mind.
Cousins, ready to back off like heifers
were staring:
                    amazed, they received
the gold funeral sovereigns she dispensed
along with talk strange to them as a sailor's parrot.

Auntie confiscated the gold;
the mourning finery, agleam with jet,
was put by to be altered. It had been chosen
by the child herself and was thought
unsuitable. She was to be
the minister's niece, now,
not her father's daughter.
                    Alone,
she would cut her way through a new world's
graystone chapels, the steep and sideways
rockface cottages climbing
mountain streets,

enquiring, turning things over
in her heart,
              weeping only in rage or when
the choirs in their great and dark and
golden glory broke forth and the hills
skipped like lambs.

The Vron Woods (North Wales)

In the night's dream of day
the woods were fragrant.
Carapaced, slender, vertical,
              red in the slant
                    fragmented light, uprose
Scotch firs,
boughs a vague smoke of
green.
          Underfoot
                    the slipping
of tawny needles.

I was wholly there,
aware of each step
in the hum of quietness,
each breath.
                    Sunlight
a net
          of discs and lozenges, holding
odor of rosin.

These were the Vron Woods,
                    felled
          seven years before I was born,

          levelled,
                    to feed a war.

Inheritance

Even in her nineties she recalled
the smooth hands of the village woman
who sometimes came from down the street
and gently, with the softest
of soft old flannel,
soaped and rinsed and dried
her grubby face, while upstairs
the stepmother lay abed bitterly sleeping,
the uncorked opiate bottle
wafting out sticky sweetness
into a noontime dusk.
Those hands, that slow refreshment,
were so kind, I too,
another lifetime beyond them,
shall carry towards my death
their memory,
grateful, and longing
once again to feel them soothe me.

Nightingale Road

How gold their hair was,
and how their harps
and sweet voices called out into the valley
summer nights!

The boys black-haired,
coming home black with coal dust, same as us all,
but milk-skinned when they'd had their wash.
One of the boys, Arthur,
went down the pit the first time
same day as me.

And the girls – that gold hair
twining like pea-vine tendrils,
and even the youngest could play her harp.

Up on the mountain, their house was,
up Nightingale Street, and then as you leave the village
it's Nightingale Road.
Mother and father, the three boys
and the six girls; all of them singing,
you'd think the gates of Heaven were open.

And funny thing –
the T.B. didn't stop them
each one, till a few weeks only
before it took them.
One by one
the whole family went, though.

Oh, but the sound was fine!
I'd be a young boy, lying awake,
and I'd smell my Mam's
honeysuckle she'd got growing
up the house wall, and I'd hear them singing,
a regular choir they were,
and the harps rippling out

and somehow as I'd be falling asleep
I couldn't tell which was the music
and which was that golden hair they had,
and all with that milky skin. The voices
sweet and gold and shrill and the harps
flowing like milk.

S Wales, circa 1890

David Lloyd

Poet and fiction writer David Lloyd was born in Utica, New York, and grew up in the Welsh community there. His articles, interviews, poems, and stories have appeared in magazines in the US, Canada and Britain, including *Crab Orchard Review*, *Denver Quarterly*, *DoubleTake*, *New Welsh Review*, *Planet*, *Poetry Wales* and *TriQuarterly*. He is the editor of *The Urgency of Identity: Contemporary English-language Poetry from Wales* and *Writing on the Edge: Interviews with Writers and Editors of Wales*, and author of a fiction collection, *Boys: Stories and a Novella* (Syracuse University Press, 2004). His poetry collection *The Everyday Apocalypse*, winner of the 2002 Maryland State Poetry & Literary Society's chapbook contest, was published by Three Conditions Press. His poem sequence *The Gospel According to Frank* was published by New American Press in 2003. In 2000, he received the Poetry Society of America's Robert H Winner Memorial Award, judged by W D Snodgrass. Other awards include a 2001 Distinguished Scholar Fulbright Award for research and lecturing at the University of Wales, Bangor, and grants from the New York State Foundation for the Arts. He is professor of English at Le Moyne College where he currently holds the Rev Kevin G O'Connell, S J, Distinguished Professorship in the Humanities.

Bedtime Stories

In the story called 'A Search for Coal',
my father as a child sits in an empty bucket,
legs over the sides, hands on the handle.
He makes a wish, closes his eyes,
and flies off like Kafka's bucket rider
above the streets of Corris.
He counts the slate shingles on the roofs
of all the houses,
buzzes sheep browsing the bare hillsides,
swoops down to a mountain of coal
that is his for the taking.
This day, the sun hangs in a cloudless sky
for three extra hours,
and no one tells the bucket rider what to do.

In the story called 'Communication',
my father is a young boy who can read minds.
He walks into the kitchen of his childhood home
on a morning when no words have been spoken
to tell his mother what it is she really thinks.
She bakes a tray of scones, lays them out
with clotted cream and blackberry jam on her best china plate,
and says in Welsh, 'these
are all for you.'

When I begin writing the story
called 'Tywyn County School',
the words get stuck:
loneliness, loneliness, loneliness.

But in the story called 'Newborn' my father takes me
from my mother's arms, holds me out in front of him,
admires my chubby face and tiny fingers,
and throws me with a great heave
high into the air
so that I rise above the trees, above rooftops, chimneys,
antennas, above the highest floor of the hospital,
and turn six slow summersaults among the birds
before floating down to him like a seed from far away.

When the writing of all stories is finished,
I use scissors to cut out every other word,
locking these in a drawer of my desk.
The other words, I read to my children before bedtime,
telling them not to worry about what is missing.

The First House I Knew

When I stand facing my father in the silent living room,
both of us trying to phrase a thought,
I glance down at my palm
and see that the life-line has lengthened.

In the dining room, my sister combs her red hair
before a gilded mirror.
Around her, hyacinths sprout from the carpet,
shoot up and bloom purple, gold, green.

One brother plays the piano in his bedroom,
repeating the same mistake, the same way,
the same eight measures.
My other brother shouts from the attic,
'Is anyone home? Is anyone
home?'

In the kitchen of the first house
I knew, my mother is singing an old Welsh hymn
at an open window without a screen. Rainwater fills
the birdbath in the yard but the sparrows flock
to a bush near the window.
'Jerusalem', my mother sings, stretching out
the syllables. 'Jerusalem.'

My brother walks from the attic
into the living room with a box camera.
Though the light is poor, he takes a photograph
of my father and me.
I am tracing my love-line with a finger.
We have not yet begun to talk.

Then it is my other brother who combs
his long red hair, smiling into the mirror. My sister
picks up her violin and walks to the attic to play.
My mother finds my father in the living room and links
her arm through his. I hear their voices
but not their words

from where I lean against the kitchen windowsill
feeling a great urge to sing. The sparrows
cock their tiny heads.

The Second House I Knew

We spoke different languages
in different rooms of the second house
I knew. My mother practiced French
in the kitchen while breaking eggs for dry soufflés.
'Oui,' she would say to any question
shouted her way.

My father kept to German
in his study, speaking to himself
of synagogues and empty streets.
The gutturals soothed his sore throat.

From the locked bathroom seeped
the deep reverberations of one brother's Laplandish nouns,
mispronounced words for water. 'Where are the verbs?'
I asked through the keyhole one day,
but he didn't understand.

A second brother trusted
the strict syntax of square roots,
their lonely divisions, insistent simplifications.
He replaced his mirror with a blackboard.

My sister skipped lessons in Spanish
to master the language of love,
took to humming librettos from her bedroom window
to boyfriends crowding on the porch:
the days of *La Dolce Vita*
when my father's door was shut.

And me? No living language
but the thin flavorings of Esperanto
so I might wander, room to room, pretending
to understand the root
of every word I heard.

London, 1962

For this photograph I travel back in time
and across the ocean and through a maze
of streets with terraced houses

to reach my aunt's home in London,
1962, in the afternoon.
I find my father where I expect him,
in the parlor, sitting on the windowsill
and gazing at the street,
the door behind him closed,
a lit cigarette between the fingers of his left hand.
Cars pass the open window.

Believing he is alone, my father
does not hear his young nephew push the door
carefully, just enough to peek around
at rolled-up shirtsleeves, rising smoke,
the long gaze outside.

My father does not know that I too
have entered the room,
wondering if he is thinking of me
as I was, or of the far-away place
where he brought his family, or of my mother
as she was, or of something too private
to be imagined.

I walk across the room,
considering light, angle, depth.
I fiddle with a meter
and a lens. My father does not notice
when I finally take the photographs:
first of him – his back,
his dark, tilted head,
then of my sly cousin, who soon pulls the door,
without the slightest sound,
almost shut, and walks quietly to the kitchen
to ask about supper.

One day, long after my father's death,
my cousin tells me what he remembers seeing.
He doesn't know what it means.
He doesn't know why he remembers.

Once Again in Remsen, NY

– for Menna Elfyn, Nigel Jenkins, Iwan Llwyd

Outside, the rotting snow of April still buries
the cemeteries, fields, and rusting trailer hulks.
Camouflaged men load guns in the woods,
and the tired streets stretch by broken chapels.
An hour beyond bloody Oriskany and the siege at Schuyler,
the Adirondack foothills have swallowed us whole.

But inside we forget about hills and history,
we retreat from the Iroquois trail.
In Stinger's bar in once-dry Remsen,
on a street as main as any you'd find
in proverbial Kansas, listen up strangers:
your money's no good in here.

Now, it's the generosity of drunks that conquers.
Ambush of the furthest away and the unemployed,
the ghosts of the emigrated Welsh. Now it's the *here*
of Remsen and the *there* of Wales collapsed on barstools.
So get ready. Open wide. They want your words,
and won't take *no* for an answer.

Nothing lasts. That's what the peeling face
of main street Remsen tells us. *We come, we go*.
Yes, we come and we go, but sometimes,
like today, somehow, we come back –
so plunk more quarters in that juke box, Iwan,
and I'll set up the Saranacs once again.

Two poems from
Father and Son
(a sequence)

The Past

Because the father wanted the son to remember
from whence he came, he lifted him
onto his shoulders, higher than the Tower of Babel.
They faced east. *There*, the father said,
pointing to green hills, dark quarries, stone villages,
including his own village, exactly as it was
when he was a boy, with his mother in the kitchen,
his brother sharpening knives on the stoop.

But the boy saw only the ocean
gray and green and blue
and heard sounds that may have been
men and women singing
but more likely was the wind
distorting the noise of seagulls
playing their usual games.

Deity

We don't know where, the father said.
Or by what means. Or to what purpose.

We don't know who or how many,
what color, what shape.

We don't know which words
or if they've been invented.

We don't know when, though some say 'always'
and some say 'never'. We can't repeat

with certainty, the word 'certainty'.
We can't erase the word 'possibility'.

We can't hope. We can't despair.
We can't say the name.

We can't not say the name.

Four poems from
The Gospel According to Frank
(a sequence on the mythic styles of Frank Sinatra)

This Way

> *'Wilt thou then, for God's sake and for mine, tell me how*
> *thou might be slain? For my memory is a surer safeguard than thine.'*
> *'I will, gladly,' said he.*
>
> — 'Math Son of Mathonwy', *The Mabinogion*
> (trans Jones and Jones)

It's not easy, Frank told Ava as they lay in bed
after too many drinks loosed his tongue,

even though she never asked,
even though she never cared. *Only this way,*

Frank explained: *Only if when preparing*
for my Sunday bath Sammy, Dino, Joey and Peter

follow me in and strip off my tuxedo then lift me
so that one foot rests on the head of a crouching

Bing Crosby and one on the rim of my gold-plated bathtub,
steaming with freshly-drawn water;

and only then if a handsome actor from Spain rushes out
of the bathroom closet waving a knife he has honed

and polished every Sunday for a year,
and only then if that year is the forty-third year

of my life, and only then if the handsome actor
releases my heart from its duties

with three quick stabs and offers it, still-beating,
to the one I love most while Bing nonchalantly

considers the horror above him and my legs quake
and my feet forget their balance and their blood.

Only then, mused Frank, *only then will I be truly killed*
rather than deeply and endlessly wounded.

All right, said Ava with a bored smile
as she reached for her drink on the night stand.

I'll see what I can do.

The House that Frank Built

Frank spent one of his fortunes
on an architectural impossibility made of glass,
with glass appliances, glass furniture, glass bedsheets,
glass glasses, glass guns.

On his first day inside, Frank looked down
at the world stretching beneath his bedroom,
and focused on a friend
behaving as badly as he'd forgotten he'd behaved
the night before with a woman
whose name he'd misplaced.

Enraged, he plunged a thumb
through the house and into the earth
to pluck out a stone that he hurled at his friend,
dividing the head from the body so cleanly
the body continued its bad habits for three more days
before understanding its end had come and gone.

The liberated head rolled according to prevailing winds,
frightening children, telling stories that didn't matter
to anyone who'd listen
until it gathered speed and altitude, increased mass,
traced the curve of the earth, shaved the tops of forests,
skipped across great lakes, pierced the highest ocean waves
and proved the earth to be as round as a bodiless head
by arriving back to its origin and entering
the house that Frank built,
smashing it to dangerous diamonds
before settling like a pet
behind his newly polished shoes.

God damn it! Frank shouted at the house that was,
at the still-talking head, at the cowering earth,
at the heavens that remained speechless
because nothing was more important than themselves.

God damn it! he shouted again.
God damn it all to hell!

Unleashed

On the field of battle, Frank played dirty,
unleashing from his armed Underworld
the dogs that don't go away.

       The Dog of the Dark Glasses,
       the Dog of the Dollar Held Back,
       the Dog of the Dreadful Scowl,
       the Dog of Gigantic Generosity,
       the Dog of the Erect Penis Close By,
       the Dog of the Erect Penis Distant,
       the Dog of Sentimental Worship of the Mother,
       the Dog of Never Forgetting,
       the Dog of the Easy Smile,
       and the terrible, terrible Dog of *Who Cares?*

Slap him, Frank ordered the waiter,
pointing at the restaurant table
where his old enemy sat and ate.

Slap his face. Slap him hard,
or else you're history.

And the waiter shuffled over,
raised his hand, closed his eyes,
swung his arm with all his strength
and felt himself shrink.

Frank nodded and smiled.
He tipped the waiter profoundly
just before the diminished nobody
disappeared from sight.

Uncreation

Like the hand of a long-dead friend,
a starling alights on Frank's vast shoulder
with news of its travels over many decades
through the dangerous world:

a naked girl running from napalm,
famine in North Africa,
Eisenhower asleep,
the universe rushing away from itself,
cornfields sown with silos –

until with a thumb and a finger
Frank reaches over
and shuts its beak. *What the hell!*
Frank yells, fixing the bird's terrified eye
with his own steely blue.
I don't remember making you.

And the starling, confronted
with its unreality,
abruptly disappears.

Sarah Kennedy

Sarah Kennedy is the author of four books of poems: *Consider the Lilies* (David Robert Books, 2004); *Double Exposure* (Cleveland State University Press, 2003); *Flow Blue* (Elixir Press Prize in Poetry Winner, 2002); and *From the Midland Plain* (Tryon, 1999). She currently holds an individual artist grant from the National Endowment for the Arts and, in 2005, was awarded a grant from the Virginia Commission for the Arts. A regular reviewer for *West Branch* and *Pleiades*, Sarah Kennedy is an associate professor at Mary Baldwin College in Staunton, Virginia.

Maps from *The Universal Magazine*

found in an 18th-century domestic manuscript,
National Library of Wales

Trimmed neat and glued upside-down in the back
of her recipe book – perhaps the author

flipped from her list of herbs for the pestilence –
rosemary, rue, wormwood, lavender,

sage – to study roads while a rabbit stewed
on the fire. Staffordshire, Yorkshire, Berkshire,

Wales. Did she travel? Probably not – the child
who watercolored the sailboat pasted

to the page after puddings would have held
her at home, and she wouldn't have known her

Norfolk paths trace Margery Kempe's pilgrim
route: Lynn, Norwich to Yarmouth, where she leapt

a ferry, headed toward Jerusalem.
The headings twice the size of the script for

Portugall Salad or How to Prevent
Miscarage, the counties lie hidden – so

many blank sheets between them and her life,
lost, at last, to plague or exhaustion or

giving birth. So many meals, so many
ailments, and no good housewife's records – three

ways to cure the gout, four methods of potting
veal – *ever* strayed far from her domestic realm.

Illumination: Mary Pearson's Recipe Book, 1755

And what was there to do in the hours
of the boiling fowl, of bread dough
swelling in the bowl? She could make

another batch of ink, dye another dress
she'd only wear on Sundays. Violet, or blue,
this time, she thought, but didn't rise

from the chair. Instead, she dipped
her quill again, having just blotted dry
her note at page 47's receipt for ginger wine:

Mrs. H uses one Lemon to each
gallon. Results approved. How many times
she'd added a flavor, a spice – cinnamon

in the rice pudding, a sprinkle of cloves
in the cake – but who had ever noticed?
He wanted his food heaped high, and, yes,

he praised her, a good wife, a fine manager
of her domain, but had he even once paused
at a bite to reflect on its difference from yesterday's

taste, the beauty of plums, preserved in honey,
glowing in a white bowl under candlelight?
Like blossoms, she mused, tracing circles in circles

in the blank space on the first page,
just above the chicken fricassee.
In and around *Mary Pearson, Her Book*,

one word to each corner, the letters' points
enveloped (though no one would ever see) like petals,
she imagined, or perhaps a woman's curves.

Louisa Morgan's Inheritance, 1793

from a set of commonplace and recipe books,
National Library of Wales

The afternoon of her mother's funeral,
the books appeared beside her bed. Weeks
yet to pass before her birthday celebration,
bu: Father had left the promised brooch as well.

Before she fastened the cameo at her throat,
Louisa penned the leather covers: *Receipt*
Book L Morgan Febuye 24th 1793
and it was not until the following day

that she thought to add *began by*
the late Mrs Morgan. Cold, her dearest
companions scolded, but they had not witnessed
her mother sit, night upon night, scratching

copies from magazines or from the women
who joined her for whist every afternoon.
The books had lain in the trunk at the foot
of her bed, and her mother wore the key

on a chain at her waist. But for all her study,
Mrs. Morgan had never known fresh veal
from spoiled, had always cooked the greens to pulp,
ignoring the good advice of Hannah Glasse,

whose *Art of Cookery Made Plain and Easy*
firmly instructed that garden things, over-
boiled, have neither sweetness nor beauty.
And there, inside the first page: gambling

debts, the cost of gloves, nothing worth the ink.
And see, *How to Keep Eggs all the Year*,
that would never do. Louisa had known
for years that the lime must be fresh from the kiln.

But where was the surprise? She had always
been her father's girl, slicing his bread
at table before he could lift his knife.
He patted her head and called her good,

and her mother paid no mind, twirling a spoon
in her coffee long after she'd sugared the cup.
The book, opened to the second page,
almost fell to pieces. Surely Louisa

would find some valuable advice, medical
prescriptions for preventing coughs, cancer,
or smallpox.   But there, in her mother's hand,
were, instead, *Proposals from a Gentleman to a Lady:*

Not old – not Young, not rich not Poor,
A good old House – & a Coach & four.
Of course, the *Lady's Answer* followed beneath:
Not old, but Young, not poor but rich

A good new House – & a Coach & Six.
Trash, it was. Her mother's sort of humor.
But who was the *Most Liberal creature of creatures*,
and who'd received a crown from her mother one March?

The woman had always been easy with money: there,
scrawled in a margin, was an entry for July the 22nd,
1758. *This Day I Began My Alowance
& am to have ten Guineas a year.*

A spoiled child she had been, and Louisa's father
swore his own daughter would leave her budget
to men, as God had decreed. Had he told
his wife as much, the night of their wedding?

Was that when she'd laid it down – that he
would never touch her books, gifts from her own
father before she married? That, perhaps,
had begun the silences between them,

her mother never quite godly enough,
nor ever quite wicked. How costly
to remain imprisoned for a child,
Louisa had overheard Mrs. Griffith

murmur once, down at the kitchen table,
while her mother laid out the cards. Now,
the next few pages – *How to Pot Vennison,
Fricassee of Rabbit* – she had wanted

these for years, but where was the pudding,
the rice one with the hint of orange? How
could her mother have wasted so much time!
A whole page to some *Lines from a Lady's Milton:*

With virtue strong as thine, had we been arm'd
In Vain the Fruit had blush'd – or Serpent Charmd
Nor had our bliss, by Penitence been bought
Nor had frail Adam fell – Nor <u>Milton wrote</u>.

Riddles, charades, more verses Louisa
could not fathom. How could she have failed
to write something of value? wondered the girl,
hugging the books to her perfectly corseted chest.

Coffin, 1749

A chest, a case, a casket . . . a pastry mould for a pie (OED)

Of course there would be gossip, the cooking
fire smoking up the flue, visible for miles
in this fine weather. What would the neighbors
think – that she could not count back seven days

to the afternoon the men laid the small
box in the ground? But, no, thought Sara Moore,
the Shrewsbury matrons would not call her
touched, but cursed for lust. A decent Christian

woman did not take on a third, even
if God had left her a widow twice
and childless. She lifted the receipt book
from its shelf and opened to *Pastrys*,

recorded in the hand of her first husband's
mother. *Work plenty of greese into your
flowr to make your coffin delicate.*
Her hands had done this work a thousand times,

and comfort it truly was. But who was there
to eat? As it had come to pass, the Lord
had made her barren from her first marriage,
the first babe gone one midnight in a bed

full of blood, the second fragile from birth,
the tiny mouth refusing to close on
the nipple. This time, the milk had soured
in her breast and while she labored for days

through fever, the hearth had sat neglected.
She woke in damp clothes to find her husband,
returned from town, tucking the chill little
body next to her heart, but it did not

thrive. All were girls, so there was a judgment
to fit their tongues, and though the parson preached
all flesh was grass, Sara knew the word
over the supper tables would be *pride*

goeth afore a fall. But what did the kitchens
whisper that summer – not many years since –
the smallpox had winged its way through
dozens of infants, yes, even first-born sons? –

the Lord giveth and the Lord taketh away.
And what of the news of earthquakes in London? –
God's will be done. But the ring she wore,
that was a sign of sin and punishment

would follow as surely as morning came after
the dark. Already the flames were hot,
and Sara was at her baking. Too soon,
they would say, did she mean to draw

him to her side again so quickly? Well,
she would choose life, casting her flour, sprinkling
cold water over the fat, kneading it
to firmness. She still could hear the old

lady – excellent teacher and lovely, even
in age – reminding her, the new young
daughter, to slice her apples thin, to pinch up
her coffin's sides to hold the sweetness in.

From *The Farm Accounts of Mrs. C. Jones*

Southwest Wales, 1792

Wheat, mostly, to David Davies,
flax to the Owens, every month
a careful list of profit
and expense. The leather, dyed
the gold of ale, still feels rich,
the brass clips still click
neatly into place. Her pantry
catalogue is filled
with jellied plums and eggs
preserved in lime, vermicelli
and chocolate enough
to last through a Carmarthen
winter. Cash on hand
for necessities unpredicted.
Look, here she has sketched
her winter work: copying
a pattern of pleats from those
on the skirt of one Miss Jeffries.
How smoothly they lay
against her slim calves
when she wore the dress
to the Christmas tea.
Not like the gloves, stitched
with intricate vines and leaves.
The light was low – the evenings
coming so early! – but even
without her spectacles, worn
by day for mild short-sightedness,
Mrs. Jones was able to count
them, all those lovely,
almost mathematical folds.

Elizabeth Sloughter's Heart

from an illustration in her recipe collection, 1771

She labeled the sketch *beef stake*, seeing
that she had depicted what looked too like
a crooked heart. *N B, when seared on the gridiron,
it must be turned perpetually.* A slash

of ink across the page split the picture,
marking the *best way* to slice the meat
off the rump. Cutting top to bottom –
a quick quill-scratch – would do if smaller servings

were needed, but chopping at the grain
was *very bad.* She knew from years watching
over the help that her kitchen would be a shambles
hours before every midday meal, but who

could worry over a bit of spilled blood
unless the flesh of the hothouse Seville oranges
was ruined before the jelly could be made?
But the new girl, it seemed, would *never* learn

to prepare meat for the master's table, would weep
like a babe when a steaming half of veal was thrown
onto the block. What waste to spend a page
on a simple drawing, but what was Mrs. Sloughter

to do? The child would have to give up
those tears. To sever, quickly and cleanly,
was an essential skill. *All mortal things*
owe God their deaths, she'd explained over the cleaver.

She'd held the small hands in place, so hard
she'd felt the pulse. Even *ladies* learned sacrifice.
What kind of woman would she become, what sort
of wife, to hold a lowly animal so dear?

Mary Owen: Home Remedies, 1712

fronds of bracken are dangerous for women with child to meddle with by reason they cause abortion . . . the country name of juniper is "bastard killer"
— Culpeper's *Complete Herbal*, 1653

Her almond macaroons, proven to plump
the flesh, tempted the most withered consumptives,
and who could refuse a taste of her cowslip wine,
famous for bringing color to a pale cheek?
Her liquorice cakes could cool a fevered throat.
Copied from a royal receipt – *Queen
Elizabeth Ever Caryd Some of these*

about her – they never failed to stop
even the *vigour of a most violent cold.*
For lifeless hair she prescribed a wash
of fresh rosemary and ale, for St. Anthony's
Fire, adder's tongue juice in fresh cream.
All found relief in the home of Mary Owen,
no body, however plagued, was turned away.

That ancient Widow Wattson, her husband sighed,
who else would endure her company? With
her sack of evil leaves and her twisted face,
a fright to any innocent child, except
when she sat, of an evening, with Mary,
whose sweet demeanor made even the parson mild.
How like a lady, to work at her cookery book

with such seeming attention to that unlettered hag.
Wattson, muttering to herself, would scarcely see.
Whenever he entered the room or brought his companions,
she closed it up – such a good wife! –
and rose to offer tea. Her puddings could cure
the worst of stomach gripes. That writing
could wait – let the witch busy her hands

with her twigs. Balm and mint, Mary had noted,
sage and sweet marjoram. Fronds of bracken –
a particular gift. Mr. Owen shook his head
and said his spouse could count herself among
the saints, but he . . . he needed some peace for this night,
not these fluttering female movements. Nodding,
Mary eased her shuffling friend to the door

and gathered the herbs; she'd press them between
the sheets he'd never open. *Receipts Pertaining
to Woman in Travail* she had begun,
minutes before he appeared. Tomorrow, these
would be added to the plants *Nurse Wattson
wishs me to have, for to use as I see Occasion.*
Cranesbill for *Cours's that wont be Stopt,*

juniper berries and milk *To Bring Away
A False Conception.* They had agreed, it was not
precisely untruth but a method, lest
the page should ever fall open under
a vulgar eye, to describe the secret liquors.
As the parables do, the old one had smiled,
veiling the words most needful to be saved.

William Virgil Davis

William Virgil Davis is Professor of English and Writer-in-Residence at Baylor University and the author of three books of poetry: *One Way to Reconstruct the Scene* – Winner of the Yale Series of Younger Poets Prize (Yale University Press, 1980); *The Dark Hours* – Winner of the Calliope Press Chapbook Prize (1984); and *Winter Light* (University of North Texas Press, 1990). He has also published essays on twentieth-century British and American literature as well as the books *R S Thomas: Poetry and Theology* (Baylor University Press, 2007); *Robert Bly: The Poet and His Critics* (Camden House, 1994); *Miraculous Simplicity: Essays on R S Thomas* (University of Arkansas Press, 1993), as editor; *Critical Essays on Robert Bly* (G K Hall, 1992), as editor; *Understanding Robert Bly* (University South Carolina Press, 1988); *Theodore Roethke: A Bibliography* (Kent State University Press, 1973), as contributing editor; *George Whitefield's Journals, 1737-1741* (Scholars' Facsimiles & Reprints, 1969), as editor. He has received various grants, prizes and fellowships, including the James Sims Prize for American Literature, three Fulbright Fellowships and a semester as Visiting Scholar and Guest Professor at the University of Wales, Swansea.

Landscape

How old the dark has become,
standing silent in these fields while
horses weave through each other's shadows.
They have come like warm rain
and run over the hills in the moonlight
and stood so long alone no one
impatient would ever notice them there.

When the wind and the winter return
the horses will still be here,
their silhouettes outlined in the pale moonlight,
standing still and silent on these hills,
or stamping, splattering snow in small spills,
the whole scene turning slowly into landscape
like our own earliest memories.

First Light

– for R. S. Thomas (in memory)

I climb the steep stone
steps, glassy with cold,
to enter the empty church.
Faint light swords through
the upper dark. No wind
murmurs. No candles burn.
No God waits there nor wakes.

Last night, quite abruptly,
it began to rain. And then,
before morning, the rain
turned slowly to snow. And
then again, before first
light, almost imperceptibly,
the snow turned back to rain.

Pilgrimage

We never knew the way, couldn't get there
for the going. All day the sky had been grey
with a light mist falling. Not knowing what

we were looking for or finding had found,
we were anxious to finish whatever it was
we'd begun, to have this day put away,

on the calendar, in the album, where if we
wanted to we could take it out later and
examine it – fixed, unchanged, framed,

defined, a piece of history, even if our own.
It comes to this: we choose the life we live.
For years now I have been carrying one

small smooth stone to a nameless shrine.

Living Away

memories of the Gower coast of Wales

1

The landscape, from the upstairs window,
could keep me busy all morning. The
rolling hills waved away through history
as far as we could see. A herd of Holsteins,
like statues, grazed on the same small hill
beyond our neighbor's barn, one wall
in need of repair, the whole roof fallen in.
A dozen wild ponies roamed the moors,
entered open gates, ate roses in the gardens.

We couldn't see the sea, just over the cliff,
but the wind drove in from it, bringing
the regular rain and the blown birds.
They floated over the moors like lazy kites.
When the tide turned, they'd swoop down
to the beach to search the sand, find what the sea
stranded.

My study window looked out
from the back of the house, to the east. I liked
the late afternoons best, sitting in shadow,
watching, as if on lookout, trying to notice
and name the most minute changes in wind
and weather, in this place where everything
interrupted itself.

2

                Nothing was nearer
than one kilometer: grocery, school, post
office, the little village library — our only
outside world. One evening, without warning,
a red setter who entered opened doors,
wandered into our living room. We couldn't
find where he was from, and kept him.
We named him *Lost*. Often, he would be gone
for days at a time, and finally disappeared for good.

With only the sea for steady company,
everything adjusted to it. This rhythm
was easily learned. On days when it didn't rain,
we'd take the short steep trail to the small
private beach, a ten minutes' walk from our
front gate. Our son would climb the cliff
to the ruined castle, then swoop down on us,
waving his flag, flashing his wooden sword,
shouting *surrender, surrender or die.*

                3

Too soon, it was time to leave. This place,
now, was more than the land of our name;
it had grown into our bones like blood,
like life itself. Still, we knew we had to go,
and so we packed our bags, turned our backs,
and went. We knew we could never return,
except, again and again, in memory.

A Far Field

The rich brocade of her gown
gleams gold in the late afternoon sun

as she walks slowly
through the musk and mud

of a field near a small village,
more than three hundred years ago.

She stops to look back
briefly, as if remembering,

and lifts her hand to adjust a strand
of wet heavy hair

fallen free from her velvet skullcap.
Then, as if drawn by memory,

she comes slowly on through the field
toward the opened window

where I watch and wait.

A Visit to the Sea

It isn't ocean here for some reason.
We stand at the seashore, half-nude
with all the others, playing the games
we play at places like this. Children
build castles in the sand or dash
headlong into the water to use the waves
for toys. Women and men together
nonchalantly change from swimwear
to street clothes and wander back
to their offices after late lunches.
No one but a visitor from a place
where there is no ocean would notice
the cliffs eating away at the water
and stones dying for something to do.

Days

How many have there been, how many will there be,
days like this, when we can walk out along
this land loved by water and watch gulls scan
the sand, dogs dig for long forgotten bones,
children laugh and play, young women tan,
boys climb the cliffs and dive when the waves
are right. The days have been like years.
Already the sea has eaten out a cave in the granite
wall of the cliff and silt filled in another leg
of water, cutting the castle off completely.
If there are messages to send, send them now.

Driving Through Wales

Driving the narrow roads
wound into the landscape
like water or blood,
seeking their own levels,
occasionally we see,
through a lapse of foliage,
gaps in the hedgerows,
or a cliff cut off
at the edge of the road,
like a gift almost,
the insistent sea,
always there, if often
in background,
reminding us that we
are as alone in this
landscape as anything
we see or imagine.

Standing Lookout Above Graves End

Tonight, the sea is calm. There is no wind.
Invent the wind. From this high cliff the rocks
beneath the rocks cluster like herds of ancient
creatures gone to stone. Nothing, now, moves
them save the sea which moves nothing. Invent
the wind. Do not stand here only to stare.
Invent the wind and let it stream through
these dead lungs, these gills gone out of use.
Invent the wind. Invent, invent, invent the wind.

Margot Farrington

Margot Farrington's two collections are *Rising And Falling* (Warthog Press, 1985) and *Flares And Fathoms* (Bright Hill Press, 2005). Her poems have appeared in six previous anthologies, including *The Second Word Thursday Anthology*, also by Bright Hill Press. Other writings include interviews, essays, and book reviews for such publications as *ABR: American Book Review*, *The Brooklyn Rail*, and *Poetry Wales*. In the early 80s, she served as director of Poets for City Schools for the New York City Metropolitan area. She has worked as poet-in-residence for many institutions. Steeped in theater – her earliest love – she has performed her poetry in combination with other media.

Work

In the smithy, I've toured her tools,
seen the sculptures of a woman
working iron in what was once the stronghold
of men, and stepping outside
take note of the terrier's
refinement: fresh dig inside
an already cavernous hole
    a crater, really,
worthy adornment for that pocked madam,
the moon

and here's the ambition of pin feathers
pushing out of a gosling's head
body hurrying towards goosedom,
grave regard of its thumbtack eyes
fastened on where we're going

past walls, past
pennywort enhancing its grip in a crack
tiny spires
commanding of me: miss nothing!
as I attempt

on the site of this mill
to imagine
the water wheel – restored –
revolving through the rush
running beneath our feet, keeping my
              balance
upon the plank I find I've
walked out on with others, loving their voices
as the stretching   thread of what they say
        (what are they saying?)
turns gossamer
and snaps.

For Sale

Mortar still tight in the
stones, but the door long bolted. Lift
hands or be stung by the interweave
of nettles in waist-high grass.
  So. How much for history?
What price for faith?

Walk round (this church
hugs itself), regarding windows
too small. Never was sky accommodated,
sunlight made welcome.
Whatever angels were spoken of
have fled and
no pigeons seek this place
though a swarm of bees – fist in chain mail –
clenches high in one corner.
  Focused: the queen's all.

  Year on year advance
until a buyer comes
blind to constraints, who has no fear
of the few dead buried here, nor feels too keenly
God was either shut in or out,
but writes a check (the sum small)
to claim the patience of this place,
these ragged hedgerows,
a morning glory: diminutive gramophone
in the silence between records.

The Lark

I'm sitting by sea's edge where geology
offers a subtle union: limestone
veining sandstone's ruddy pink.
And those notes I listen to
(shivering in the westerlies),
fall like the first I might ever have
heard, profound in this coastal place, this
theater by the sea where tide-carved
creatures of limestone
grimace or gape in awe. Invention is endless here.

A rip tide: that lark's
song ineffably sweet and bold,
loosing my hold on the hour, splaying the
deck of days backwards: faces,
susurrus of numbers laid
down on the long felt surface of life.

I am brought again to that early field
at the end of a dead end street
where the song of another bird pulls
thread through the gloss of privet,
leading me back to an osage orange, bowed,
bearing from countless children
a saddle spot burnished to lucent amber.
No time to climb,
get above this current, though there's a
moment for the tiny graveyard:
five tablets of marble, their lettering
muffled in moss. Whoever is
singing now lets me lay a quick
flower down: one only for the five before the

current rushes me on, for music
swells unceasingly
from the singer's throat,
sweeping me back: I grow younger and smaller.
Buckled in a stroller, I
point at sight of a bird,
powerless yet to engrave with English,
to cut into air that word,
though if I uttered words now
they would be those venerable two
shaken out from the folds of a folk tale,
        question
endlessly asked of the traveler:

      Whither away?   No answer –
only song flashing through
space. I'm an infant babbling a string of
under notes in reverse, vanishing
into the mouths of my
mother and father
caught in a kiss, lost in the welter and
sway of 5 a.m. lovemaking
        wherein
lies the dark flare. The possibility of
me.

Crosscuts: St. Teilo

(Two riding mowers in attendance)

   No gardeners need apply.
For this insolence of grass you
need drivers, gasoline.
We'll ride those masses down
with regulated passes.

      •

Upon faces of celtic stones
lichen imitates old friends:
snowflake   flower
cloud concealing its inner cloud.

      •

Our scythe's a pair of strimmers.
Hand clippers? Strictly history.
Yew and yew and yew:
get back against the wall.

      •

Who last cat-footed to the clerestory,
past saints in leaded glass? This sunlight
stains you, seeker, into wearing motley:
a slippage harking back as far as
14th century. Whose gaze might you dare
meet? And what do you read there:
forgiveness or melancholy?

Once this churchyard relied upon
teeth of sheep. Later, some gardener.
Think how long it took him, while with
us it takes just an hour.

   Let me remind you, began the quatrefoil
   carved above church door. Surely a splendid
       speech,
   lost to the doubled roar of mowers.

Selkie

A single line would occupy him for many days.
– Vernon Watkins,
Letters of Dylan Thomas to Vernon Watkins

Ah yes, the single line.
From where I attempt to write this
she suns herself at a distance,
sleek upon rock, beautifully blent
with that warm shade. The stretch of
sea between us. Oh, keel furrowing sand, you
make too obvious
    my intent. But I have embarked.

My dory leaks. I carry with me my usual
flask of tears. (Rarely a swig, friends,
rarely a swig). I've a fish sandwich and always,
my inability to swim. Something ails the left
    oarlock, makes my rowing sore, and the sun –
beset by mist – in sullen alchemy makes lead
from waves that earlier shone

pewter. My prow hammers; I'm
aware the line has changed, lovely as I am
awkward; I'll never catch her this way.
My net has holes, it was ever thus,
yet must I row for a glimpse. One look of
recognition, cruel as any club.

    She left – in slipping off – the darkest spot
upon the rock. I fend off. The mist thickens.

    Yet I have known her now, and I
know nothing. Fathoms and fathoms she swims
as I row back. Swash of the shallows, cold about
my ankles. I've a grain of sand between
two molars, and I grind it there. One bubble escaped
from her mouth has somehow entered my ear.
A month may pass; a night will
come, whitely illumined,
and in another form she will be
given me on shore.

Joseph Clancy

Joseph Clancy is a native of New York City but has lived in Aberystwyth since his retirement in 1990. He is Marymount Manhattan College's Emeritus Professor of English Literature and received his Ph.D from Fordham University. His recent books include a collection of poems, *Ordinary Time* (Gomer, 2000), *Other Words: Essays on Poetry and Translation* (Univeristy of Wales Press, 1999), and translations of *Medieval Welsh Poems* (Four Court Press, 2004).

The Visitors

We have it easy. Wales ends for us
With the close of the book, the crossing of Severn,
To revive with a magazine photo, a letter,
An overheard accent.

If for some its prospects, its weathers surface
Unpredictably under other skies,
A comfortable grief, content to have invented
A world we can long for.

The painter departs the hillside: his canvas holds
Fields, farmhouse, ploughman, in a lucid instant.
Within the valley's misted frame the farmer
Gets on with his sowing.

The Graves

St. Michael's, 1961

Each day in Aberystwyth
We walk to and from our room
A pathway through a churchyard
Where long grass, no close-clipped turf,
Grows, and the gravestones tender
Their legends of fact and love.
Place of sea-air and sunlight,
Its stillness never a hush
Of reverence, merely a small
Companionable quiet,
No voice is ever silenced
Passing through, but children laugh,
Lovers chatter, and the dead
Preserve their peace untroubled.

Where are our dead? This summer,
A week's sea-voyage away,
We are no further distant
Than we are when we're at home.
My grandmother's bones lie in
A field like a parking lot,
Merely one mound of many,
Unthought-of, unvisited.
A hand that I do not know
Tends to the grass, the flowers
Are placed each week by proxy,
And the dead stay out of reach.

This small Welsh town possesses
The art of ease with the dead.
Yesterday in the churchyard
An old man, browned by the sun,
Was mowing among the graves.
He doffed, a cheerful reaper,
His cap, and said good morning
As we passed on our daily walk
New-mown grass on the gravestones
Spilled green, and the air was sweet.

At Sunset

– for Meic Stephens, 1984

"What? All these times in Wales
And never seen the Valleys? There's an hour or so of light left –
Let's go now."
                                        And so a 90-minute drive in the past tense
Beneath the greening Rhondda tips,
The poisoned land topped now and then by regimented pines,
Along the single street of houses bound to houses, village bound to village,
Like Siamese clones.
Park Road through the Rhondda Fawr abruptly stopped –
Three wooden garages barred the deep drop sudden as a pitfall:
Beyond, the bleak beginnings of the Beacons.

The miners are out once more this spring,
Not for a higher price on black-flecked breath
But for slower closures, an extenuation of extinction.
"Not for ourselves," one said on television,
"But for our sons." Keep the pits open
To claim the children? The shaft of his imagination opened on no other
Source of food and shelter, core of neighbourhood.

A reel of places – Hirwaun, Dowlais, Merthyr –
Whose names blaze clearer than their car-blurred images.
Across a crest, past this dry spring's fire-blackened pines,
And down. In the hillside opposite
A habitat whose name we can't remember snaked
Bright-buildinged, hugging the convolutions of the rock.
And then upon a stretch of road from which we looked
Down on a small and undistinctive sprawl, the usual houses, churches, shop
Another stop, although this road wound on.
"There it is," you said. "That's Aber-fan."

128

We stared across for a numb moment at the present schoolhouse
                              like a yellow tombstone below,
The 116 children's graves.
The stubborn gorse flared spiked and golden from the rock-face.

Orange lights along the road flicked on like head-lamps
As we sped down to Cardiff in the coming dark.

Museum Piece

The Museum of Welsh Life at St Fagans

It is like walking through an elegy.
   The rhythms of the paths in shade and sunlight
String visitors along a facile stroll

Through bakehouse, farmhouse, schoolhouse, tannery,
   Smithy and gorse-mill, cruck-barn, kiln, and chapel,
To eighteenth-century gardens and the castle.

Everything's authentic here, and as unreal
   As china bridges in a home aquarium.
The buildings float within a reservoir

Of antiseptic memories, detached
   From a community to serve. Nothing
Is fed here but the sweet tooth of nostalgia

By currants in a well-baked funeral cake
   (Commemoration that pays loving tribute
And comforts that the past is safely dead),

And foreign appetites for passing through
   A mummy neatly wrapped. Slate quarries in Ffestiniog,
Coal pits in the Valleys, and soon perhaps Port Talbot's

Steel Works – will all Wales be saintfaganized
   To pump our tourist dollars through Welsh veins
And keep a Welsh heart going in the ICU

Of a picturesque folk park? A nice place
   To visit, but you wouldn't care to live there.
After a day's diversion on these paths

It helps to recall a cowshed's healthy stench
   On a working farm near Brecon, the racket
Of a noonday crowd in Carmarthen market,

And the bubbling Welsh of a two-year-old in Cardiff
   To her uncomprehending grandfather's welcoming ears.
It is too easy to write elegies in Wales.

Tourists

Natural, the plaint that visitors by visiting
Spoil what they visit for. We change a place
By entering. It enters us, and changes.

This too is natural, the hankering for elsewhere:
We leaf through brochures, scan the travel shows,
And spin the globe's kaleidoscope. We step

Outside our ordinary time, invent
The luxury of being transient, duty-free
Observers underneath a foreign sky.

Strangeness like beauty's in the eye
Of the beholder. Naive our gaze – the native's
Commonplace is our exotic. We must read

The text without the context; complexity
Gets lost in our translation. Never mind.
Redefined by otherness, refreshed

By differentiation, we return
As strangers. We re-enter
Our common places. They enter us, and change.

Margaret Lloyd

Margaret Lloyd was born in Liverpool, England, of Welsh parents but grew up in a Welsh community in central New York State. She received a Ph.D from the University of Leeds, England, and has published a book on William Carlos Williams' poem *Paterson* (Fairleigh Dickinson University Press, 1980) and two poetry collections: *This Particular Earthly Scene* (Alice James Books, 1993); and *A Moment in the Field: Voices from Arthurian Legend* (Plinth Books, 2006). She received a fellowship to Hawthornden Castle – an International Retreat for Writers in Scotland – where she completed *A Moment in the Field*. Currently, she chairs the Humanities Department at Springfield College, Massachusetts.

They are not here but I think of them here

The mist is a line of ghosts drifting
westward over the still water

to congregate at the end in a cloud of witnesses.
I dream this lake is the ocean

we crossed from Liverpool to New York harbor.
I was two years old, there was sea for eight days.

We arrived with thirteen trunks,
a one-ton crate of furniture.

People in my family have died and are still
dying across the ocean. So many ghosts

between me and the far shore.
Water laps against the rowboat.

I turn and see the lilies are open.
This is America. This is the state of Maine.

Every day I memorize details:
Yarrow is the brightest flower before the dark comes.

When the crows stop screaming,
small birds can be heard.

I remember the furniture that came with us:
a carved oak sideboard and dining room table,

granddaughter clock with two chimes,
glass-fronted bookcases.

Another country and another
language lived in our house.

I now can see to the other side,
but can't penetrate the stand of trees.

The mist is lifting but the ghosts still drift.
This is the somewhere else I have always been.

Near the Shore

I like these rocks which change
every day with the sea.
Clear pools of water in reefs
with fish swimming in them.
The cormorant in the harbor
floating alone. I like
this rock which fits my foot
as I rest from the way
small rocks hurt.
My eyes enjoy looking
at the woman who spots two
wild black swans in the sea.
She can't take her eyes off them
as she walks along the pier.
Bryn finds a dark stone,
gives it to me,
and asks over and over
why I like it. I say
because it is round, smooth
with a perfect white circle
and he found it for me.
I like the way late afternoon
mountain shadows darken
the sea near the shore.
And knowing in this moment
that no one
with my blood is hurting.

The Organ Player

A young man with nothing on his feet
plays the organ inside the church.
She sits outside on the slate gravestones
listening to the music, thinking
of his large hands and the way last night,
her back cold against the castle wall,
he put one hand over her eyes
and the other over her head
while he kissed her mouth,
using it completely because it was all
she would let him use.
Now he plays a requiem by Fauré
and practices the hymns for Sunday.
She thinks of the sea nearby and its insistent roar.
And then of the small water running
down the Cambrian mountains, finding
its way around rocks, ferns, the roots
of ancient trees. How distinct that sound is.
How everything can be heard at the same time.

Line of Yellow

– for my father

I want to tell you now that my children
have painted land and sea you loved,

those sands you walked on, with a line
of yellow between the blue of the sea

and blue of the sky, so that sea and sky are always
separate, though constant in their blue.

One Christmas I was given two tea sets –
one a delicate bone china.

I played only with the common set
you gave me. I was loyal

in my sermons to neighborhood children
and my prayers at night.

Tonight I remember
that at the end you, too, faced

the complexity of inconstancy. David told me
on your deathbed you asked our mother for a kiss.

Her heart stretched one way and her body another.

Law and Grace

After my grandmother died, no one was allowed
to drink from the cup in which he brought her tea
every morning or sit in her chair near the fire.
I was forbidden to play cards on the cold floor
of the front parlour where her body had been laid out.
I remember endlessly rolling clay
between my small fingers to make flowers
for the Garden of Eden while thinking of the paralysis
which had begun in her throat, her total silence
for two years before her death.

Years later, I believed when I heard a poet say
angers are not fatal angers, that silence is fatal.
I now know words as well as silences destroy and redeem.
Every day there is the possibility of confession or denial.
I yearn to have no choice – involuntary sounds of love-making,
inevitability of water rushing out of a bucket
turned upside down. I have never been able to live
under the law and I can't tell when I live under grace.

I do know that when I lived along the sea,
sometimes the sun went down so quickly,
if I turned my back I could miss it. Its being gone
was as final as anything could be.

What She Knows

It is life and death. Her seriousness drives her
out of the wooden cabin in Vermont to stand
in the violence of a wind forcing leaves to expose
their paler sides, lifting Iroquois Lake
in a multitude of waves toward heaven
like the bodies of lovers in fierce bliss.
Small bluets strain with their mouths
full of each unexpected and relentless breath.
But she knows there is a wind apart
from the way it moves the world.
On Pumlumon mountain in Wales
where there are no trees and the grass short
from the grazing of wild sheep, she had felt
the wind blow, and blow violently
in her exposure, her own long hair
over and beyond her face, coloring
the world a deep red.

Cardigan Bay

Our eyes scan the horizon, to the north,
the south, and then more closely
along the line for any darker shapes
that signify a boat or an island.
The horizon is as empty as it is full,
history catching up with us. I want
to drink until after the lights have gone on
then off along the promenade,
until after the gulls begin to sleep
with their heads on their sides,
and the multicolored houses no longer
end in me. When our children see
our emptiness, we have to know it
for ourselves. The sea reflects nothing,
has no room for this lowering, brooding sky.
For months the god in me has not spoken.

Six poems from
A Moment in the Field: Voices from Arthurian Legend

Merlin Speaks of Nineve

Love can bury us alive and still we follow it.
I followed her all over Cornwall and Wales
and into France, teaching all I knew,
showing her the hidden and wonderful places.
Still she would not let me enter her.
But sometimes she would kiss me,
near a river streaming with cress or standing
by a high falls in Wales, the water dark
brown from peat bogs after heavy rains.
And strangely it was enough.
I could at any point have used my craft
to open the door to her astounded heart,
but I was beyond having to prove myself.
I did not come to her the way God came
to the young Jeremiah and touched his mouth.
Every secret she learned, she learned one by one.
When the moon was most full, we caught
the outgoing tide through the vale of Usk.
In Cornwall, I showed her the last thing
I would show her: the most dark
she would ever see, darker than earth
after the death of the moon, darker
than any grave. Then she left, rolling the stone
over the entrance, leaving me permanently
inside her. The only sound I hear
is water dripping from the rock.

She Speaks of Merlin

He followed me out of Camelot
but I returned alone. Everything
I learned, I learned from his mouth.
We left little trace as we passed –
bent reeds near the shores of Bala,
remains of fires by the Irish Sea.
His lips like low mist drifting over the moors.
The world disappeared.
We left little trace as we passed –
small whinberries missing from their stalks,
bits of fabric caught on wild brambles.
Everything I learned, I learned from his mouth.
Inside and outside are the same,
a mouth is where a river joins the sea.
We all know that someday we will die,
but he knew how and when.
Loving me was loving death.
We left together, but I returned alone.

Merlin Imprisoned in the Cave

I have been a white hart and a wild man,
have spoken with pigs and counseled kings,
rested in the tops of trees, watching

geese leaving with the moon.
Even so I was overcome by love
the way sleep sometimes overcomes us

in the late afternoon. I stand here bent
and listening to water dripping
from the rock, wondering, even now,

what it means to love what we know
will never love us. But we choose her
anyway, following her even here

where I must bow my head
to drink out of the hand of oblivion.
In the final sleep there is no room

for dreaming, no room for thinking.
But I want to think of the great silence
of the wild geese even with their loud cries

and of dry leaves scattering in the wind at night.
I want to think of Lancelot, of Gawain, and of Arthur
who this very night ransacks the court seeking my counsel.

I stand here bent and recalling the voices
of the dead and of those who will die soon,
as if I am trying to remember a dream. I want

to think of the world I made and then walked out of
after her. Wherever I turn my eyes, wherever I look,
I see the black ruins of the world collapsing.

Morgan Heading Toward Trouble

Lately I've been thinking about Efnisien.
The trouble-maker, the rash prince, the complicated man.
I see him in the north of Wales.
It's the dead of night,
everyone exhausted from feasting.
He slashes the lips, tails, and eyelids of horse
after horse until all the King of Ireland's
steeds are maimed for his revenge.
In the dawn, he leans back to rest
against the toadflax growing in the castle walls.
I find myself heading toward that kind
of trouble. Wanting to disrupt the feast,
overturn the order, throw a child
into the fire to avenge some insult.
And later be perfectly willing to break
my heart for any necessary reason.

Guinevere Lies with Arthur

I woke up thinking there is no life
after death, despite mounds,
burial chambers, things made
only for the dead, all the appeasement
of ancestors, a child buried
with his head pointing to the rising sun.
All night I listened to the sound of ropes
banging against masts in the harbor
like a hundred small drums. And I lay
in bed this morning with his mouth
on my breast while the long curtains
moved slowly in the wind. The gray
of the day bled into blue as I turned
my body on his dark chest
and buried my head in his neck.

Arthur's Hands

I do not live, as some say, content with order and shape.
I want what I want and hold it against our fates,

not allowing myself to know what I can plainly see,
the air charged with her cries of love.

Where does the knowing go? Minute by minute
there is nothing that needs to be known.

When I wake in the morning, I look at my hands
and think of what they can do, how they grasp and give,

their strength with steel and without.
Once I was led to the lake. I saw the shadows of the birds fall,

the sky brooding on the surface of the rippling water.
Mistakes and the depths are everywhere.

Achilles' own body betrayed him.
The war will come, and after – silence.

Any one of us, given certain circumstances, could be king.
Distant, set apart, never drinking the dregs but always the clear wine.

I admit everything to myself,
whispering into my large hands at night.

Anne Stevenson

Anne Stevenson was born in Cambridge, England, in 1933. Of American parentage, she was brought up in the United States and attended schools in New Haven and Ann Arbor, taking her BA from the University of Michigan. In 1961, she took a Master's Degree in English from Michigan but since then has mainly lived and worked in Great Britain. Oxford University Press has published nine collections of her poetry, including *The Collected Poems, 1955-1995*. Her collection *Granny Scarecrow* was shortlisted in 2001 for the Whitbread and Eliot Prizes. In 2002, she was awarded Britain's largest literary prize, the £60,000 Northern Rock Writer's Award. A recent collection, *A Report from the Border* (Bloodaxe Books, 2003) was followed in 2005 by *Poems 1955-2005* (Bloodaxe Books). Having served as writer-in-residence in Dundee, Oxford, Edinburgh and Newcastle, Anne Stevenson has written extensively on Sylvia Plath and Elizabeth Bishop. She lives with her huband, Peter Lucas, in Durham and north Wales.

Anne Stevenson

Anne Stevenson was born in Cambridge, England, in 1933. Of American parentage, she was brought up in the United States and attended schools in New Haven and Ann Arbor, taking her BA from the University of Michigan. In 1961, she took a Master's Degree in English from Michigan but since then has mainly lived and worked in Great Britain. Oxford University Press has published nine collections of her poetry, including *The Collected Poems, 1955-1995*. Her collection *Granny Scarecrow* was shortlisted in 2001 for the Whitbread and Eliot Prizes. In 2002, she was awarded Britain's largest literary prize, the £60,000 Northern Rock Writer's Award. A recent collection, *A Report from the Border* (Bloodaxe Books, 2003) was followed in 2005 by *Poems 1955-2005* (Bloodaxe Books). Having served as writer-in-residence in Dundee, Oxford, Edinburgh and Newcastle, Anne Stevenson has written extensively on Sylvia Plath and Elizabeth Bishop. She lives with her huband, Peter Lucas, in Durham and north Wales.

Anne Stevenson

'A Present' appeared in *Granny Scarecrow* (Bloodaxe Books, 2000); 'Binoculars in Ardudwy' appeared in *Four and a Half Dancing Men* (Oxford University Press, 1993); Section II of 'Green Mountain, Black Mountain', 'May Bluebells, Coed Aber Artro' and 'Without Me' appeared in *A Report from the Border* (Bloodaxe Books, 2003).

A Present

– for Lee Harwood

A grey undecided morning.
No wind.
It's cold, so get dressed quickly.
Step out into the new born air.
Look around.
It's yours, this shifting misty envelope,
a hospital to breathe in,
along with chaffinches and great tits
queueing for the wire feeder;
on the lichened wall beneath,
dunnocks make do with titbits.
Now a thrush in concentrated rushes
combs the pasture.
Those sheep-bitten daffodils
poke up, you'd say, out of nowhere,
though moles know
what's going on down there,
rebuilding under their slagheaps
a secret city.

But your secret's up in the hills,
so pull on your socks, boots, woolly hat
and layers of windproofing.
Fill up your thermos, shoulder your pack.
The ice age planed these mountains down for you
too many millennia ago to be

reasonably thanked.
They're a gift like your life,
that never thought to be a life.
Moelfre, Rhinog Fawr, Y Llethr, Diphwys,
bald monitors bearded with cloud,
at rest in their Welsh nomenclature.

And like living things, old.
So old they're not likely to look older
when one day you don't remember them;
when lovers and readers you can't know about
get up at six or seven on chill winter mornings
to greet them, choosing, maybe,
certain words of yours to remember you.

Here's a present, the gift of a perfect view
straight back to a future that,
despite the computer, won't change in a hurry.
Shall I tell you what happened
in mid-February, 2099?
A soft cloud clung to the summit of Foel Ddu.
The next day, thickening, it crept down,
and as the wind backed to the east,
veered south, west and north-west,
hail, sleet, sunburst and snow flurry
gave pleasure to a lonely walker, cold
but happy on the high ground,
as the sun handed him a hillside,
bright as ever green moss
shone over stone in the bronze age.
The story in the marsh was a long memory
retelling itself in a shower of gold.

Binoculars in Ardudwy

North Wales, 1990

A lean season, March, for ewes
who all winter camped on the hills.
They're gathered in now to give birth
to children more cheerful than themselves.

There's a farmer, Land Rover, black dog
trotting, now rolling on his back.
At the gate, sheep bunched – one alone
drifting down the steep Cambrian track.

Look now, the sun's reached out,
painting turf over ice-smoothed stone.
A green much younger than that
praises *Twll-nant* and *Pen-isa'r-cwm*.

All this through the lens of a noose
I hold to my focusing eyes,
hauling hill, yard, barn, man, house
and a line of blown washing across

a mile of diluvian marsh.
I see every reed, rust-copper,
and a fattened, S-bend of the river.
Then, just as I frame it, the farm

wraps its windows in lichenous weather
and buries itself in its tongue.
Not my eyes but my language is wrong.
And the cloud is between us forever.

Under cover of mist and myth
the pieced fields whisper together,
'Find invisible *Maes-y-garnedd...*,
Y Llethr...Foel Ddu...Foel Wen.'

May Bluebells, Coed Aber Artro

No Greek self-pitying hetairos in blue-rinse curls,
the north's true Hyacinthus non-scriptus
(much written about, nonetheless),
    beloved of Hopkins, who in Hodder Wood
perfectly caught its 'level shire of colour'
    while his companions talked.

West Country 'Crowfoot' or 'Grammer Graegles',
    in Welsh translated 'Cookoo's Boot',
'Blue of the Wood', 'Welcome Summer',
    each silky delicate bell-stalk
carrying its carillon to one side,
    dusky wine-cups, ringers of creamy anthers,
in *Cymbeline* misnamed 'the azured harebell'
    by Arviragus...

And even in our time,
    self-assigned to resurrection.
Camping gas set burning
    at the lowest visible flame.
Ice-age giant still nourishing
    the trodden mulch and green enchantment
of his daughter beechwood, watering
    one more summer out of hazy veins.

From Green Mountain, Black Mountain

II

In Border Powys, a Land Rover
stalls on a hill track.
Dai Morgan climbs out with a halter,
plods to a sodden field where
a mare and her colt have mauled
the wet soil of Welsh weather
all a mud-lashed winter.

Unlatching the gate, he
forces the halter on the caked,
anxious head of the mare,
then leads her away to where
a plan of his own makes fast
to some spindle purpose
the fate of the three of them.

The inscrutable movements of the man
puzzle the horses, who
follow him, nevertheless,
up the piebald track
snowdeep in drift in places,
tyre-churned with red mud.

These are the Black Mountains
where the drenched sleep of Wales
troubles King Arthur in his cave,
where invisible hankerings of the dead
trouble the farms spilled over them –
the heaped fields, graves and tales.

And Dai, with his brace of horses,
nervous of strangers, inbreeder of races,
is Teyrnon still, or Pryderi the colt-child,
fixed without shape or time
between the ghost-pull of Annwfyn,
that other world, underworld, feathering
green Wales in its word-mist,
and the animal pull of his green dunged boots.

Without Me

A north wind light this morning.
Who will watch it
gilding the hennas of the marsh?
Between the iron gate's upright
and its top rung
death's in her diamond collar.
And if ewes last night
laid glistening pebbles, the pasture
will be pointillist with dung,
with burnished dung-flies busily feeding.

After heavy rain, a flood of sun,
but not for me the rainbows hanging
one   one   one
from lines of crooked fencing
that will rust by noon.
Now what's that shadow by the pigsty
pecking, looking, pecking?
Fly away, silly bird, fly!
Whose pasture will be grazing
on your white bones soon?

Notes

Wiliam Greenway

'Halloween in Wales'
    'Little Orphant Annie' – a poem by James Whitcomb Riley, which
    inspired the American comic strip 'Little Orphan Annie'.

'At Arthur's Stone'
    Simmer dim: the Scottish name for the longest day of the year –
    the summer solstice, June 21.

'The Train to Neath'
    Knacker's yard – a slaughterhouse.

Jon Dressel

'Synopsis of the Great Yanklo-Welsh Novel'
    This poem refers to Welsh poet Harri Webb's comic poem,
    'Synopsis of the Great Welsh Novel'.

    'Welcome in the Hillsides' – a sentimental song in the order of
    'Come Back to Erin'.

    'Hen Wlad fy Nhadau' (Old Land of my Fathers) – the Welsh
    National Anthem.

'Dai, Live'
    Prytherch – a Welsh peasant figure in the poetry of R S Thomas.
    Thomas announced Prytherch's death in a poem in 1966.

    Dai, short for Dafydd (David) – a generic nickname for Welshmen,
    as Paddy is for Irishmen.

The Investiture – Charles Windsor was invested as Prince of Wales in 1969, an event derided by Welsh nationalists.

'A Bedtime Story'

This poem refers to the legend of Madoc, a 12th Century Welsh Prince who is supposed to have sailed west and discovered America, landing near what is now Mobile, Alabama. He and his followers were said to have intermarried with the Native Americans and founded a tribe of Welsh Indians. The legend has it that he did return to Wales, once.

Deganwy – the fortress of Llywelyn the Great, which he destroyed rather than let the English occupy.

Cilmeri – the Welsh village near which Llywelyn ap Gruffydd was killed in 1282.

Glyndŵr raised his standard at Corwen, north Wales, on September 16, 1400. For a time he made his seat of power the castle at Harlech.

Since the Tudors were of partly Welsh descent, Henry, Earl of Richmond's defeat of Richard III at Bosworth Field in 1485 was seen by the Welsh as fulfillment of the ancient bardic prophecy that a true Briton would one day regain the kingship of the island. Things didn't work out as foretold, as the Tudors quickly became thoroughly Anglicized.

Mawddach – a major river of north Wales.

Hydref – October.

'Note from a Soldier'
Historical evidence suggests that Arthur was an early 6th Century Romano-British cavalry leader (not a king) who fought battles in what is now Wales, south-western England and southern Scotland, and who inflicted a great defeat on the Saxons at Mount Badon (probably near the city of Bath in Somerset), stopping their westward advance for fifty years. By the time the romancers finish transmuting the story, Arthur had become King of England, whereas the historical Arthur was the enemy of the ancestors of the English.

'Two Hoots for a Huntress'
This poem refers to the legend of Blodeuwedd, in the Fourth Branch of *The Mabinogi* – the great collection of Welsh tales written down in the early Middle Ages but which are much older. Blodeuwedd was made from the flowers of the oak, broom and meadowsweet by the wizard Gwydion, to be the bride of his nephew, Lleu. She betrays Lleu, however, and with her lover Gronw Bebyr, conspires to kill him. Lleu is not killed but is changed into an eagle, which his uncle Gwydion later finds 'rotting' in a tree and cures by reciting a series of *englynion* (stanzas). With the help of Gwydion, Lleu exacts revenge upon his unfaithful wife and her lover. Gronw Bebyr is killed by a spear which passes through a stone behind which Lleu has allowed him to take refuge, and Gwydion transforms Blodeuwedd (her name means 'flower face') into an owl.

David Lloyd

'Bomber Over Carreg Cennen'
Carreg Cennen – a ruined castle in south Wales.

'Once Again in Remsen, NY'
Oriskany and Fort Schuyler – American Revolutionary War battle sites in upstate New York.

Saranac – a beer made in Utica, New York.

'This Way'
This poem draws from the story of the attempted murder of Lleu Llaw Gyffes in the Fourth Branch of *The Mabinogi* (see note to Jon Dressel's poem 'Two Hoots for a Huntress').

'The House that Frank Built'
In 'Branwen, Daughter of Llyr' – from the Second Branch of *The Mabinogi* – the head of Bendigeidfran is able to exist without its body and converse with friends for eighty-seven years.

'Unleashed'
Arawn, Lord of the Underworld, appears with a pack of hounds when Pwyll and he first meet in the First Branch of *The Mabinogi*.

'Uncreation'
The communication between the bird and Frank Sinatra draws from the Second Branch of *The Mabinogi*.

Margot Farrington

'Work' and 'For Sale'
The water-wheel and the church mentioned in these poems are in Merthyr Mawr.

'The Lark'
The poem's locale is Rest Beach in Porthcawl, south Wales.

The American 'stroller' would be a 'pram' in Wales.

'Crosscuts: St. Teilo'
St. Teilo's 14th Century church possesses a fine old churchyard with ancient stones and yews. Many yews live for centuries and the yew is associated with immortality.

A 'strimmer' would be a 'string mower' or 'weed whacker' in the United States.

'Selkie'
In Celtic mythology, selkies traditionally straddle two worlds. By day they are seals but at night they swim in to shed skins on the beach and take human form. If a woman loses possession of her sealskin to a mortal man, she is bound to him, tied to life on land unless she can get her skin back.

Anne Stevenson

'A Present'
Dunnock – a Welsh sparrow-like bird.

'Binoculars in Ardudwy'
Ardudwy – a county in Wales.

Y Llethr, Foel Ddu, and Foel Wen – ancient hills in the Rhinog chain.

Maes-y-Garnedd, Twll-nant, and Pen-isa'r cwm – sheep farms/ farm houses in Cwm Nantcol.

'May Bluebells, Coed Aber Artro'
Hetairos – Greek for a boy lover.

Arviragus – a character in Shakespeare's play *Cymbeline*.

'Green Mountain, Black Mountain'
   Teyrnon and Pryderi – characters in the First Branch of *The Mabinogi*. After preventing a mysterious creature from kidnapping his prize colt, Teyrnon finds an abandoned baby who proves to be Pryderi, son of Pwyll, Prince of Dyfed.

Acknowledgements

Joseph Clancy
'At Sunset' and 'Museum Piece' appeared in *Here & There* (Headland, 1994); 'The Graves' and 'The Visitors' appeared in *The Significance of Flesh* (Gomer, 1984); 'Tourists' appeared in *Ordinary Time* (Gomer, 2000).

William Virgil Davis
'A Far Field' appeared in *Hampden-Sydney Poetry Review*; 'A Visit to the Sea' appeared in *Kansas Quarterly*; 'Days' and 'Standing Lookout Above Graves End' appeared in *Southwest Review*; 'Driving Through Wales' appeared in *Bogg*; 'First Light' appeared in *Borderlines*; 'Landscape' appeared in *The New Criterion*; 'Living Away' appeared in *The Sewanee Review*; 'Pilgrimage' appeared in *Christianity and Literature*.

Jon Dressel
'A Bedtime Story', 'Children, Night, Llansteffan', 'Dai, Live', 'Dai on Holiday', 'Note from a Soldier', 'Note to a Character', 'Synopsis of the Great Yanklo-Welsh Novel', 'The Holy Well', 'Two Hoots for a Huntress' and 'Why I Live in Llansteffan' appeared in *Out of Wales: Fifty Poems 1973-1983* (Alun Books, 1983).

Margot Farrington
'Crosscuts: St. Teilo', 'For Sale', 'The Lark', 'Selkie' and 'Work' appeared in *Flares and Fathoms* (Bright Hill Press, 2005).

William Greenway
'At Arthur's Stone', 'Fancy View', 'Llyn y Fan Fach', 'Power in the Blood', 'The Train to Neath', 'Welsh Courier Braves Daylight' and 'Worm's Head' appeared in *Simmer Dim* (University of Akron Press, 1999); 'Halloween in Wales' appeared in *Ascending Order* (University of Akron Press, 2003); 'Otherworld' appeared in *Twice Removed* (Main Street Rag, 2006); 'Pit Pony' appeared in *Where We've Been* (Breitenbush Books, 1987).

Sarah Kennedy

'Coffin, 1749' appeared in *Chautauqua Literary Journal*; 'Elizabeth Sloughter's Heart', 'Illumination: Mary Pearson's Recipe Book, 1755', 'Maps from The Universal Magazine' and 'Mary Owen: Home Remedies, 1712' appeared in *Prairie Schooner*; 'From the Farm Accounts of Mrs. C. Jones' appeared in *Virginia Quarterly Review*; 'Louisa Morgan's Inheritance, 1793' appeared in *The Southern Review*.

Denise Levertov

'An Arrival (North Wales, 1897)' and 'The Vron Woods (North Wales)' appeared in *Candles in Babylon* (New Directions, 1982); 'Inheritance' appeared in *Door in the Hive* (New Directions, 1989); 'Nightingale Road' appeared in *Life in the Forest* (New Directions, 1978); 'The Sea Inland' appeared in *Sands of the Well* (New Directions, 1996).

David Lloyd

'Bedtime Stories', 'London, 1962', 'The First House I Knew' and 'The Second House I Knew' appeared in *The Everyday Apocalypse* (Three Conditions Press, 2002); 'Deity' and 'The Past' appeared in *Stone Canoe*; 'Once Again in Remsen, NY' appeared in *Planet*; 'The House that Frank Built', 'This Way', 'Uncreation' and 'Unleashed' appeared in *The Gospel According to Frank* (New American Press, 2003).

Margaret Lloyd

'Arthur's Hands', 'Guinevere lies with Arthur', 'Merlin Imprisoned in the Cave', 'Merlin Speaks of Nineve', 'Morgan Heading for Trouble' and 'She Speaks of Merlin' appeared in *A Moment in the Field: Voices from Arthurian Tradition* (Plinth Books, 2006); 'Law and Grace', 'Line of Yellow', 'Near the Shore', 'The Organ Player' and 'What She Knows' appeared in *This Particular Earthly Scene* (Alice James Books, 1993); 'Morgan Heading for Trouble' first appeared in *Planet* under the title 'Heading Toward Trouble'.

Anne Stevenson

'A Present' appeared in *Granny Scarecrow* (Bloodaxe Books, 2000); 'Binoculars in Ardudwy' appeared in *Four and a Half Dancing Men* (Oxford University Press, 1993); Section II of 'Green Mountain, Black Mountain', 'May Bluebells, Coed Aber Artro' and 'Without Me' appeared in *A Report from the Border* (Bloodaxe Books, 2003).